Retire Abroad

Practical books that inspire

Taking a Year Out
Opportunities for employment, study, volunteer work and independent travel

Getting a Job in Canada
Secure a well-paid job and a great new lifestyle

Getting a Job in America
How to find the right employment opportunities and contacts

Getting a Job in Australia
Secure well-paid work and a great new lifestyle

Getting a Job Abroad
The handbook for the international jobseeker

For full details, please send for a free copy of the latest catalogue:

howtobooks
3 Newtec Place, Magdalen Road,
Oxford OX4 1RE, United Kingdom
email: info@howtobooks.co.uk
http://www.howtobooks.co.uk

Retire Abroad

Your complete guide to
a new life in the sun

ROGER JONES
2nd edition

how tobooks

By the same author

Getting a Job Abroad
Getting a Job in America
Teaching Abroad

British Library Cataloguing in Publication Data.
A catalogue record for this book is available from
the British Library.

Published by How To Books Ltd,
3 Newtec Place, Magdalen Road,
Oxford OX4 1RE, United Kingdom.
Tel: (01865) 793806. Fax: (01865) 248780.
email: info@howtobooks.co.uk
http://www.howtobooks.co.uk

First edition 1993
Second edition 2002
Reprinted 2003

Produced for How To Books by Deer Park Productions
Typeset by PDQ Typesetting, Newcastle-under-Lyme, Staffs.
Printed and bound by Cromwell Press, Trowbridge, Wiltshire

Contents

Preface

If you are planning to retire in the near future or have already done so, this is the book for you. Retirement brings with it so many advantages. You are no longer bound to a strict work routine and can make use of your newly found freedom to indulge yourself a little.

However, just because you are retired does not mean that you are old. You are not yet of an age when you are content to sit back and reminisce about the past. Instead you are determined to live life to the full and fulfil as many of your aspirations as you can. These may well involve spending time in a different – probably warmer – clime for part or even all of the year.

But how does one set about turning these dreams into reality? *Retire Abroad* offers suggestions and advice, and also provides a wide range of contacts – from estate agents to embassies, from furniture removers to financial advisers. Such assistance could prove crucial, since moving abroad is not without its pitfalls. It is essential to investigate carefully before taking the plunge.

As the number of British pensioners living abroad approaches the million mark, I am delighted to have an opportunity to undertake a complete revision of this book which first appeared in 1993 under the title *How to Retire Abroad*. The reference section has been extended and updated, and I have introduced a section on immigration consultants and lawyers which will be of particular interest to anyone hoping to retire to countries of the English-speaking world which now impose stricter immigration controls.

I hope that this new version will prove an indispensable guide in your decision making, raising points you may have overlooked and steering you successfully in the right direction. However, I cannot emphasise too strongly that because individual circumstances differ greatly, it is only possible to offer general pointers in the pages of this book. I therefore recommend that before you venture into the unknown you seek out as much advice as possible specific to your own situation. It is vital to look before you leap.

Unfortunately, no book of reference can claim to be completely up to date. Organisations come and go; addresses and telephone numbers seem to alter with increasing rapidity; laws change, particularly those relating to immigration, social security and taxation. So you should never hesitate to contact the relevant authorities and professionals for the very latest information, a chore now made somewhat easier thanks to the technological wizardry of the Internet.

Nor can a book of this size be all-embracing. I have concentrated on the countries which are currently the most popular destinations for either retirement or long-stay holidays. But this selection should not inhibit your choice. Countries such as Croatia, Bulgaria and the Scandinavian countries have much to recommend them, and for the adventurous there could be possibilities in the Pacific region or parts of Latin America.

I am, incidentally, always pleased to receive suggestions that might be incorporated into future editions of this book. I also trust that this volume will help you to reach the right conclusions and that you will enjoy a full and rewarding retirement.

Roger Jones

ACKNOWLEDGEMENTS

It would have been impossible to write this book without the assistance of a number of people in the UK, Spain, Cyprus and elsewhere who have given generously of their time to offer me suggestions and answer questions.

I am particularly grateful to FOPDAC, NAEA, John Howell and Co. and Outbound Newspapers for the help they have given me in the revision of this book.

1

The Third Age Dawns

'Retire' according to *Chambers Twentieth Century Dictionary* means 'to withdraw; to retreat; to withdraw from society, office, public or active life, business, profession, etc; to go into seclusion or to bed'.

This hardly describes the lifestyle of most of the retired people I know. Many lead very active lives travelling, playing sports, studying, participating in club activities, gardening, doing voluntary or part-time work. Now that they no longer have to concentrate on earning a living they expend their energy on things they enjoy doing. The last thing they want to do is curl up and have a nap.

NEW ATTITUDES TOWARDS RETIREMENT

Over the years in western countries the nature of retirement has changed. It is no longer seen as a time for reflection and inaction, and there are several reasons for this.

Life expectancy

'One of the greatest achievements of the twentieth century has been to add over twenty years to the average age expectancy (at birth) of British people,' notes Professor R A B Leaper. 'To survive into "old age" is no longer a bonus for a small minority of people, but an experience common to the majority.'[1]

In the past most people were lucky to reach retirement age, and even those who did were often too old and decrepit to enjoy it. Now the average 60-year-old man can expect to live another 16 years at least, and a woman of that age can look forward to celebrating her eightieth birthday. A 65-

year-old man can reasonably plan to live another 13 years, and a 70-year-old another ten.

Improved health

Thanks to improved healthcare, health awareness and diet, people in their sixties and seventies are on the whole fitter and healthier than their forebears. Even those who experience health problems are more likely to surmount them thanks to medical progress. A retired person can expect to retain his faculties far longer than ever before, and even when they become defective medical technology can often provide a solution.

As a result more retired people than ever are capable of leading very active lives. Far from being content to sit back and watch the world go by, they want to play a full part in it, prepared to meet fresh challenges and filling their lives with a wide range of activities, including sport.

Early retirement

People are retiring earlier. For some public service employees retirement at 55 seems to be becoming the norm, and it seems that 70% of private sector workers finish work by the age of 60. Fewer than 60% of British men in the 55–64 age group are still in employment. The concept of early retirement is even more entrenched in France where only one-third of 54–64 year olds are actively employed.

Many of these early retirees are in the prime of life who in different circumstances would be leading busy lives perhaps at the top of their trade or profession. Some look round for other work and even embark on new careers; others who feel financially secure seek outlets for their energies elsewhere.

Prosperity

Although the image of the hard-up pensioner persists, an increasing number of people now on the threshold of retirement are actually quite well off. Some 'woopies' (well off older people) have inherited wealth from their parents; others may have benefited from the rise in house prices and sold a large family home for a considerable profit; many will have substantial occupational pensions or investments that yield a good return.

'Woopies' are not inhibited by lack of finance. Indeed, they may well find themselves better off than earlier in their lives when they may have had to cope with heavy mortgages and support a growing family.

Greater expectations

With better health and increased wealth people are able to choose how they wish to spend their retirement. They have a chance to fulfil some of the ambitions they have put aside, to embark on activities they have not had sufficient time for up till now, such as hobbies, travel or study.

Although ambition is regarded as the prerogative of younger people, there is no reason why it should be abandoned as a person advances in years. Today it is not uncommon to hear of people in their late fifties and sixties setting up their own businesses or taking up new jobs. Indeed, in Britain 15% of new businesses are started by people aged 50 plus. There is no reason why you should not plan ahead and decide what you wish to achieve by the time you are 60, 70 or 80.

MAKING A FRESH START

An increasing number of people make a clean break by selling their house and retiring to another part of the country – often the seaside or the countryside.

There are certain gains from a move. 'With a new house in a new place and subsequently a new circle there can come a new energy which breaks into new interests often with more forcefulness than that which inaugurated our working days, for we still retain the poise given us by the seniority of the work from which we have just retired' (Ronald Blythe).[2]

In the past, towns like Bournemouth, Eastbourne, Torquay and Worthing became favoured retirement locations earning the south coast of England the nickname 'Costa Geriatrica'. But certain inland locations, like the Cotswolds and the various spa towns, are also popular. Generally speaking, people who move do so because they want

- a better climate – better is normally synonymous with milder or warmer, though clean, fresh air free of pollution can be an important draw;

- to get away from the crowds – for many older people the ideal spot is far away from the noise, bustle and pollution of the big city, hence a home in the country or in a small town is a popular choice;

- a healthier environment – a resort or the countryside is generally healthier than an industrial region, and people suffering from respiratory complaints will benefit from living in a drier, milder climate.

Other factors which influence the choice of retirement locations are:

- past connections – people may wish to move back to an area where they have strong emotional ties. This may be a place where you once lived or where you have stayed on holiday;

- family ties or friendships – if friends or members of your family (eg your children) have settled in another part of the country, you may decide to move nearer to them.

THE LURE OF FOREIGN PLACES

British people have always had a reputation for globe-trotting, but until fairly recently the actual number of people who ventured abroad of their own accord was fairly restricted. All that changed in the late 1950s with the introduction of cheap package tours and charter flights to southern Europe.

Holidaymakers quickly discovered that resorts in Spain and Greece were considerably sunnier and warmer than Torquay and Bognor Regis. There were other advantages too, such as cheap wine and spirits, exotic food and a more relaxed way of life.

As people found property and land going for a song they began to acquire holiday homes. Estate agents in the UK began to market overseas properties, while property developers, including a number of British firms, started to put up purpose-built residences to cope with demand. Short stays grew into more extended ones, and people began to think in terms of permanent settlement. As a result there are now tens of thousands of British citizens living on the Spanish costas alone.

The idea of spending one's retirement outside the circle of one's family and friends is a symptom of the age we live in. 'The growth of retirement migration reflects not only the growth of affluence but also the increasing emphasis is our societies upon individual satisfactions and expression, and the changing conception of family responsibilities and of inter-generational support,' writes Dr Anthony Warnes.[3]

There is, of course, nothing new about living abroad. At any given time there are hundreds of thousands of British people living and working abroad – in the services, in the diplomatic service, in education or development, on construction projects, representing their firms – the list is endless.

Some stay abroad for a short spell and then return home; others relish the life in a particular country or region so much that they endeavour to stay on into retirement. Citizens of the world who spend their careers moving from country to country do not necessarily head for their country of origin when they retire. They are seasoned expatriates who are content to settle down anywhere provided the circumstances are right.

However, many of the people who retire abroad these days after spending most of their working lives in Britain have only a vague notion of what long-term residence abroad entails. A short period spent in another country, on holiday or business, does not always prepare one for the business of transplanting yourself permanently to foreign soil.

PLANNING AHEAD

Moving to a foreign location is not a simple move. It is more akin to starting a new life or embarking on a journey. As any explorer will confirm, any long-term expedition needs to be planned with scrupulous care; you must be prepared for problems along the way, and above all you need to be flexible in your attitudes.

'It is not easy to start a new life in a foreign country, no matter how many times you have visited that country or how much you love it,' observes Susan Thackeray.[4] 'Emigration is a traumatic experience... and the older you are the more difficult it is to discard the habits of a lifetime and take on new ones.'

So it is sensible to think long and hard before committing yourself to an overseas retirement. Among the factors you need to consider are:

- your health – you may be fit and healthy now, but there may come a time when your health is less robust;

- your finances – you may be flush with cash at present, but more often than not people become poorer as they grow older;

- your retirement location – you need to ensure that the country and location you select is as wonderful and trouble-free as it appears in the brochures;

- your family and friends – you ought to consider the impact your decision might have on others, including members of your family and close friends.

I have heard of numerous instances of people who have flown down to the Mediterranean for the first time and bought a retirement home on impulse. While some may have lived happily ever after, others have encountered pitfalls. Costs escalate, the glamour wears off, they have a contretemps with the taxman, one partner dies, their health deteriorates, and so on.

It is to help you avoid these pitfalls and get off to a good start in your adopted homeland that this book has been devised.

REFERENCES

1. Leaper, RAB: Introduction to the *Policy Studies in Ageing* series (Centre for Policy on Ageing).
2. Blythe, Ronald: *The View in Winter* (Allen Lane).
3. Warnes, Anthony M: *Migration after Retirement: Occasional Paper No 12* (Department of Geography, King's College, University of London, June 1981).
4. Thackeray, Susan: *Living in Portugal* (Robert Hale).

2

Thinking Things Through

Going to live abroad represents a major decision whatever one's age, and you need to consider carefully from the outset whether it is the right course of action for you. For the young and unattached moving to another country is a relatively simple matter, but for others who are well established in a particular locality, it can represent a considerable upheaval and expense.

Is it worth it? Living abroad may sound exciting, even glamorous, but one really needs to look beyond the enticing brochures. A warm, mild climate, for instance, may be an ideal breeding ground for mosquitoes, and the summer temperatures may prove overwhelming; picturesque villages may lack vital facilities that you take for granted, especially if your health is poor; and although the social life promises to be enjoyable, do you really want to be separated from family and friends at your stage of life?

Seasoned expatriates who have lived and worked abroad for a number of years will have some inkling of what to expect and be accustomed to examining the pros and cons of living in a particular country. This is something that you must get down to as well, and this chapter sets out a range of matters that you need to consider.

THE THIRD AGE AND BEYOND

I have referred to the fact that people – in the developed world at least – are living longer and staying fitter. Indeed retirement for some can represent a considerable chunk of their lives which can be divided into three distinct phases:

- The active, independent phase. You are in full possession of your faculties and are fit and healthy. You also have sufficient retirement income. Most people who consider retiring abroad are in this condition, ready to live life to the full – and this phase could last for ten, twenty or thirty years, depending on circumstances.

- The less active, partly dependent phase. Unfortunately, increased age takes its toll, and you may find yourself entering the next stage. Your health may start to fail, you may experience the death of a partner or need someone (usually a relative) you can turn to in an emergency.

- The dependent phase. This is the time when you are no longer able to cope by yourself. In the UK there are a wide range of welfare facilities to help you cope with the problems of age which come in the form of home helps, meals on wheels, sheltered housing and residential homes.

I don't want to sound excessively gloomy. A good many people remain in full possession of their faculties until their final hours, and for a retiree in the peak of condition the idea that some day one could be 'sans teeth, sans eyes, sans taste, sans everything' will sound positively grotesque.

However, you need to bear in mind that a sudden illness or disability can strike down the fittest pensioner. We are fortunate in the UK that there is a comprehensive system of services, both statutory and voluntary, to ensure that the elderly disabled are properly looked after.

Elsewhere in the world health provision is less extensive and not really geared up to dealing with frail expatriates. In Spain, for instance, care for the elderly tends to be the responsibility of the family or charities (normally religious orders), and sheltered housing for expatriates is still comparatively rare.

PERMANENT OR TEMPORARY FOREIGN RESIDENCE?

In view of the fact that your health is almost bound to decline in time, you may decide against settling abroad permanently. Instead, you might opt to limit your stay in another country and return to the UK when you start to become frail or your partner dies.

This is quite a sensible plan, though it does not always work out in practice. People rarely recognise that they have moved on to the second or third phase of retirement, and they put off the evil day when they have to change their lifestyle. It is not really surprising, since returning home can represent a considerable upheaval in itself: it means abandoning your circle of friends, a familiar lifestyle and often an attractive climate to return to the leaden, unwelcoming skies of Northern Europe.

Even if you make up your mind to return to Britain there could be obstacles in your path. In recent years overseas property owners have experienced difficulty in selling their homes, or have returned to the UK only to find that houses have become so dear that they cannot really afford one with the anticipated receipts from the sale of their foreign property.

One solution is to keep your feet in two camps as it were, and live abroad for just part of the year. Like a migratory bird you winter in Florida or Southern Europe and return to the UK for the spring and summer. Maintaining two residences might sound expensive, but some of the cost could be offset – at least partially – by letting either dwelling at the times of the year when you do not need it.

At this point it is worth noting that the decision to live indefinitely in a country may not be entirely in your hands. Would-be retirees to the USA, for instance, may find a permanent residence visa is difficult to come by, though it is perfectly easy for a foreigner to buy a home there and stay in it for a substantial part of the year on a tourist visa.

YOUR DEPENDENTS

The working phase of your life is over and you are keen to
start afresh. Other members of your family may be in a
different position, and you need to consider their feelings
before you make plans that are likely to affect them. You
clearly need to discuss the implications of a move with them
and work out whether they should accompany you or not.

Your partner

When a couple retires abroad, it often happens that the wife
has greater difficulty in adjusting than the husband. Various
reasons have been suggested for this including the change of
life, difficulty in striking up new friendships, new domestic
arrangements, homesickness or the very fact of having a
husband about the house all day. Separation from friends,
children and grandchildren can cause anguish. On the other
hand, some couples move so as to be nearer their children.

Your children

By the time most people come to retire, their children will
have left the family home and be leading independent lives
of their own. However, there will be some who for various
reasons (eg a late marriage, early retirement) still have
children of school age.

An important consideration will be their education.
Although this will not be too much of a problem if you are
retiring to an English-speaking country or a place where
there are expatriate English-medium schools, elsewhere you
may need to consider other options:

- a local state school – this is fine in an English-speaking
  country, but if your children do not speak the language
  of the country they could be at a disadvantage, though at
  primary school level this is less of a problem;

- an English-medium school in your country of residence –
  most schools of this nature, whether they are boarding
  or day schools, charge fees;

- a boarding school in Britain – this would work out even more expensive, though some local educational authorities can provide boarding facilities;

- correspondence tuition – the courses on offer from Mercers College are expressly designed for expatriate children;

- teaching them yourself – this is possible using the facilities of the WES Home School;

- leaving them with relatives or friends in Britain to continue their education – this is a sensible option if they are coming up to important examinations. Of course you may decide to delay taking up residence abroad until these examinations are over.

If you want your children to go on to higher education in the UK, you need to bear in mind that if they are resident abroad, they are unlikely to be eligible for subsidised student loans.

Elderly relations

Some people have elderly parents or other relatives who are reliant on them to a certain extent – to do their shopping, to get their pensions, to manage their financial affairs. Even if they are quite capable of living independently, they may be accustomed to regular visits and invitations to your home.

Some elderly relatives may be keen to relocate with you – and if they are fit and active, why not? Older ones, however, are more likely to want to stay put. Clearly, you will need to consider their position carefully and explore a number of possibilities, such as

- retirement homes
- sheltered housing
- accommodation with friends or other members of the family
- a home help or live-in companion.

Your pets

There are few problems in taking pets abroad provided they have pet passports with the required vaccination certificates before they go, including anti-rabies injections if you are off to mainland Europe and certain other countries (see Chapter 7).

But some pets are like some wines: they do not travel well, especially over long distances. You may love the sun, but furry Fido may find the heat overwhelming, while Felix prefers more familiar haunts. Besides, some separation may be involved with countries such as Australia, New Zealand and Cyprus imposing a period of quarantine on arrival.

YOUR HOME IN THE UK

The question to consider here is whether to retain your UK residence or sell it.

Retaining a UK base

Some would-be expatriates want to maintain a home base and perhaps spend time in Britain each year. Indeed, a survey by Surrey University found that 20% of retirees in Spain still owned a property in the UK. However, under present tax regulations there is a penalty to pay: if you maintain accommodation for your use in the UK you will remain a UK resident in the eyes of the Inland Revenue and therefore still be liable to pay UK tax.

If you leave your home empty for any length of time, there can be problems. A house can deteriorate quite rapidly if it is not lived in, and there is a danger of it being broken into or taken over by squatters. You may well have to appoint an agent to keep an eye on it, while your insurance company may have qualms and either increase the premium or refuse to insure you.

There is a way out of this dilemma: you can let your home, and then regain possession of it when or if you return for good. Make sure, however, that you draw up a tenancy agreement that will enable you to do this – an assured shorthold tenancy or an assured tenancy. Even then, you may have to apply for a court order to evict a tenant who does not want to move.

Selling up

Often people decide to sell up completely in order to finance the purchase of a home abroad. Such a move might serve to convince the Inland Revenue that you are no longer resident in the UK for tax purposes (see Chapter 6) and with luck result in a cash surplus that you can invest.

Selling up could act to your disadvantage if you decide to return to the UK and need to begin the house-hunting rigmarole all over again. Problems can occur if in the intervening years house prices have risen more in the UK than in your country of residence and you find that the sum you raise from selling your foreign residence is small in relation to the price of a house in Britain.

YOUR FINANCIAL HEALTH

Can you afford to buy a property abroad and, if so, will you have enough to live on? Financial problems are the last thing you want during retirement, and you therefore need to investigate thoroughly the financial ins and outs of retiring abroad. You need to get an estimate of:

- the total cost of buying a residence including taxes and professional fees;
- the cost of moving your personal effects from one country to another;
- the likely running costs of your home (including service charges if you are in an apartment block);
- the various taxes you will have to pay (eg rates, wealth tax, income tax).

You could also find that your travel expenditure escalates, particularly if you and your family make regular visits back to the UK. You may find that insurance premiums are higher than in the UK. Living costs have a tendency to increase over the years and if your income does not rise in line with these costs, you could live to regret the move.

A large part of this book is concerned with financial matters, and this is no accident. As a pensioner you are unlikely to find ways of boosting your income if prices increase. Most pensioners find their real income either remains steady or slowly diminishes. In Britain there is a financial safety net in the form of supplementary benefits, but you cannot count on having access to a similar system abroad. Generally, you will need far more than the basic British state pension to make ends meet.

STAYING ON

If your career has taken you overseas, you may feel inclined to stay on in a country where you have spent a significant portion of your working life. You are, after all, used to the place and should be well equipped to cope.

Whether this is a sensible option or not depends very much on the country. Staying on in the Bahamas is a very different matter from staying on in some poverty stricken township in Africa. In the latter case no matter how much you love the people and the country, if you are no longer able to make a contribution to the community because of failing health, you risk becoming a burden to the very people you want to help.

A DIFFERENT SOCIAL ENVIRONMENT

'There's no place like home' goes the old song, and many people are genuinely attached to the UK no matter how much they may complain about it. Can this attachment be transferred to another country which may have different social customs, a different ambience, different attitudes, maybe a different language? Would you be able to cope when the novelty wears off?

A few retirees imagine that life on the Mediterranean is just like living in Britain but with sun added. This is a mistaken belief, even if you are living in a largely expatriate environment, and you could become irritated or frustrated by little things, such as no milk deliveries, the difficulty in obtaining your favourite food items, or the lack of decent TV programmes.

Things are bound to be different: the water supply may be unreliable; there may be frequent power cuts; the telephone system may be antiquated. You may discover the nationals of the country have strange habits of which you disapprove. The place may turn out to be too darn hot in July and freezing in January.

As frustrations mount up your retirement is unlikely to prove the happy, comfortable time you have been looking forward to. To avoid making a dreadful mistake you need to get to know a place really well before you put down roots, and make certain you can adapt easily to your new surroundings. Why go off to be miserable in Crete when you can lead a much more contented life in Crewe?

GOING TO LIVE WITH OTHER PEOPLE

If you have suffered a bereavement or succumbed to a serious illness, you may well receive invitations from your children, other relations or friends to move in with them. Such an arrangement can work out very satisfactorily in the UK. But what if they live thousands of miles away in a country with which you are not familiar – in Canada or Australia, for instance?

If you have little or no experience of living in other countries or prefer to stay independent, you should guard against hasty decisions. By all means go to stay on a temporary basis, but do not dispose of your home immediately. Then, if things do not work out, you have somewhere to return to.

3

Choosing a Location

When you are working you have to live in an area in striking distance of your place of employment. As a retired person you will be free of such constraints. You have the luxury of being able to make up your mind where to live and of taking time to reach your decision.

Unless you have robbed a bank and need to make a quick exit from the UK, there is no sense in rushing off to the first place that comes to mind. You may have a pretty shrewd idea of where you would like to settle, but you have only seen the area during the season when it is at its best. If you are considering becoming a permanent resident, you need to find out what it is like at other times of the year.

Take the weather, for instance. Temperature and rainfall statistics can be a useful guide, but they do not tell the whole story. A wet weekend in Marbella can be just as miserable as one in Manchester, and your favourite spot in the mountains may turn into a quagmire after a storm. The Mediterranean can be pretty rough at times, hurricanes can wreak havoc in the Caribbean and Florida, and some areas of France are prone to flooding.

Even if you have set your heart on one particular area, I suggest you keep other options up your sleeve, just in case you cannot find the type of property you want there at a reasonable price. If you have no success in Spain, you could look at neighbouring Portugal. If you find the coast is overdeveloped, you might venture inland away from the main holiday centres.

This chapter is designed to set you thinking about possible locations.

PHYSICAL LOCATION

An island

Islands have always been popular holiday venues; perhaps it is because we are all Robinson Crusoes at heart. However, there are islands and islands, and some of them might prove too small for comfort or too isolated. Malta, for instance, with its 95 square miles is half the size of the Isle of Wight; Bermuda is little more than 20 square miles in area. Fortunately neither can be termed isolated since they enjoy good airlinks with the rest of the world – which is more than you can say for St Helena and some South Pacific islands. On the other hand Cyprus, Corsica (France) and Sardinia (Italy) are sizeable territories.

Car owners also need to bear in mind that the cost of transporting their vehicle to the mainland by ferry can mount up.

The seaside

Coastal resorts have always been popular retirement locations; you have only to think of Eastbourne, Bournemouth and Torquay in the UK. All of them are geared to the holiday trade, but many are all-year-round resorts with a substantial permanent population. Others are full of holiday homes that remain vacant for most of the year and some may shut down completely out of season. In the high season resorts tend to be crowded with holidaymakers, and wily residents head out of town. Many prefer to live at some distance from the sea in order to avoid the summer crowds.

The countryside

Some people prefer the peacefulness of the countryside and look for old farmhouses and cottages in picturesque surroundings. Tuscany and Umbria in Italy are deservedly popular, tumbledown properties in rural France find ready buyers in the UK, and people are starting to move away from the Spanish coast into the hills. A place in the country can be very pleasant, but may lack the full range of amenities. In more isolated areas your own transport is essential.

The city

Inveterate city dwellers enjoy the entertainment and cultural offerings that only a large city can offer. Even when the weather is foul there is something to do in Paris, Madrid, Lisbon, Rome and Vienna, and there are smaller cities such as Dublin, Florence, Venice and Seville which can be very attractive to live in. The advantage of cities is that you have everything at your fingertips; on the other hand, property is usually more expensive and the cost of living higher than elsewhere.

The mountains

Spectacular scenery and fresh mountain air are a considerable attraction. For the energetic there may be the possibility of winter sports when the snow is on the ground and mountaineering in the summer. However, as you grow older you may well prefer winter warmth to winter snow and find you lack the energy to negotiate steep slopes.

OTHER CONSIDERATIONS

Cost of living

This is an important consideration when you are living on a fixed income. You may be attracted to a location because of its relative cheapness. However, you should not assume that prices will remain low forever, especially if an area undergoes extensive development as happened on the Spanish costas.

It is a useful exercise to look at prices in local shops and work out how much it would cost to live in the area. You also need to investigate the cost of electricity, water and the telephone, and find out what taxes you will have to pay. Try to get hold of a cost of living report – from the Embassy of the country itself, the local British consulate, the Women's Corona Society or an expatriate self-help organisation.

You may well find it hard to generalise about prices. Some will be higher than in the UK, especially imported goods; local products will normally be cheaper. If you aim to lead a lifestyle identical to the one you led in Britain, you may find that living is far from cheap; but if you modify your tastes to accommodate local practice, you will make a considerable saving. Abandon pickled onions, porridge and pork pies in favour of pizza, pasta and paella on the Mediterranean and you will make substantial savings.

Climate

The idea of sunshine all year round may sound attractive, but is this really what you want? Many people enjoy the change of seasons and might find living in the tropics somewhat monotonous. There may be unpleasant features in the climate of your favoured location which you may have overlooked (eg dry winds, excessive humidity, occasional hurricanes).

You need to consider your health. For instance, will you suffer from respiratory problems if the climate is too dry or too wet, or if the atmosphere is too rarefied? Is your skin sensitive to prolonged exposure to the sun? If you have any doubts you should consult your medical adviser before you go any further.

The climate charts in this book will give you an idea of what to expect in various locations around the world. Many of the places mentioned are not very much above sea level, and you need to bear in mind that nearby locations at higher elevations (say, 1,000m above sea level) may be cooler in summer and colder in winter.

While temperature and hours of sunshine will doubtless be of greatest interest, the other information on rainfall and humidity is also relevant. Low rainfall plus high temperatures could mean an arid landscape at certain times of the year. High temperature and high humidity make for an oppressive atmosphere.

Currency fluctuations

How strong is the currency of the country where you wish to settle? Bearing in mind that the pound can fluctuate in value against other currencies, this is important for anyone whose pension is paid in sterling. When the pound is strong you will feel like a millionaire; when it is weak in relation to other currencies your money will not go so far.

In the early 1990s British pensioners living on the Continent experienced a loss of income when the pound was devalued against other European currencies, but more recently they have benefited from a much stronger pound. If, as anticipated, the UK eventually adopts the euro, currency fluctuation in Western Europe should become a thing of the past, but it is an issue which you should not ignore in countries further afield.

Consider the USA. If the pound is worth $1.50, living in the USA is relatively cheap for anyone whose income is in sterling. If the pound drops to $1.20 your pound will buy 20% less. This is why if you decide to retire to a country with a strong economy, it may be prudent to have your savings in a number of different currencies, rather than keep all your cash in a sterling account.

Cost of property

Some areas are more popular than others and this is reflected in the price of properties. If money is no object you will be able to think in terms of a villa in Cannes or St Tropez; otherwise you would do better to explore areas which are less popular or which have yet to be discovered.

However, the purchase price is not necessarily the end of the story. There may be extra costs to consider; purchase tax, maintenance costs, local taxes, etc. If you opt for a flat in a complex with a swimming pool and gardens, for instance, there could be a hefty service charge to pay which might increase over the years without a corresponding rise in your personal income.

There is a firmly held belief that property is a good investment which always appreciates in value, but you cannot count on this happening. If the property market is booming, you may be lucky enough to sell at a considerable profit, though in some countries you may have to pay capital gains tax. When there is a slump in house prices you may find that you do not even recoup your initial outlay on your residence.

RAINFALL CHART
(Average monthly precipitation in millimetres)

	JAN	FEB	MAR	APR	MAY	JUN	JUL	AUG	SEP	OCT	NOV	DEC
UK: London	54	40	37	37	46	45	57	59	49	57	64	48
Andorra	34	37	46	63	105	69	65	98	81	73	68	69
Australia: Sydney	89	102	127	135	127	117	117	76	74	71	74	74
Austria: Salzburg	76	64	71	91	130	167	195	166	109	82	71	64
Bermuda	107	87	109	106	114	97	112	143	146	162	116	114
Canada: Toronto	66	58	66	66	71	63	74	61	66	58	63	61
Canaries: Lanzarote	28	19	16	7	1	1	0	1	5	5	23	26
Cyprus: Nicosia	90	52	36	16	13	4	1	1	3	33	49	106
France: Marseilles	43	32	43	42	46	24	11	34	60	76	69	66
Greece: Athens	62	37	37	23	23	14	6	7	15	51	56	71
Ireland: Dublin	67	55	51	45	60	57	70	74	72	70	67	74
Italy: Rome	71	62	57	51	46	37	15	21	63	99	129	93
New Zealand: Christchurch	59	43	48	48	66	66	69	48	46	43	48	59
Portugal: Faro	70	52	72	31	21	5	1	1	17	51	65	67
South Africa: Cape Town	17	13	24	60	97	105	98	83	49	40	19	15
Spain: Alicante	20	20	18	40	31	12	4	14	46	52	36	25
Switzerland: Geneva	63	56	55	51	68	89	64	94	99	72	83	59
USA: Miami	51	48	58	99	163	188	170	178	241	208	71	43

TEMPERATURE CHART
(Average maximum daily temperatures – Celsius)

	JAN	FEB	MAR	APR	MAY	JUN	JUL	AUG	SEP	OCT	NOV	DEC
UK: London	6.3	6.9	10.1	13.3	16.7	20.3	21.8	21.4	18.5	14.2	10.1	7.3
Andorra	5.9	7.3	12.3	14.2	16.9	23	26.1	24.2	21.8	15.6	10.3	5.8
Australia: Sydney	25.5	25.5	24.4	21.6	18.9	16	15.5	17.2	19.4	21.6	23.3	25
Austria: Salzburg	1.6	3.7	9.3	13.8	18.5	21.9	23.5	23.1	20	14.1	7.6	2.7
Bermuda	20.2	19.3	20.1	21.9	24.4	27.2	29.7	30.3	29.1	26.5	23.7	21.2
Canada: Toronto	−0.8	−0.1	3.9	11.8	18.2	24.2	27.2	26.3	21.6	14.7	7.4	1.1
Canaries: Lanzarote	20.9	21.3	22.7	23.3	24.6	25.7	28.1	29	28.5	26.3	24.5	21.8
Cyprus: Nicosia	16.4	16.9	18.8	22.9	27.6	31.6	34.3	34.4	32.2	28.4	22.9	18.5
France: Marseilles	10	11.5	15	17.9	21.8	26.1	28.9	28.3	25.1	19.8	14.7	10.9
Greece: Athens	12.9	13.9	15.5	20.2	25	29.9	33.2	33.1	29	23.8	18.6	14.6
Ireland: Dublin	7.6	8.2	10.4	12.7	15.4	18.4	19.6	19.4	17.3	13.9	10.3	8.4
Italy: Rome	11.1	12.6	15.2	18.8	23.4	27.6	30.4	29.8	26.3	21.5	16.1	12.6
New Zealand: Christchurch	21.1	20.5	18.9	16.7	13.3	10.5	10	11.1	13.9	16.7	18.9	20.5
Portugal: Faro	15.3	16.1	17.5	19.7	21.9	25.2	28.2	28.2	25.7	22.4	18.9	16.2
South Africa: Cape Town	26.4	26.6	25.8	22.6	19.7	18	17.2	17.9	19.3	21	23.5	25.2
Spain: Alicante	15.7	17.2	19.1	21.3	24.4	28.3	31.1	31.5	29	24.5	20.3	17
Switzerland: Geneva	3.6	5.5	10.4	14.8	19.1	22.9	25.2	24.4	20.5	14.3	8.3	4.4
USA: Miami	24.3	25	26.6	28.1	29.7	31.1	31.6	32.1	31.1	29.3	26.8	25.1

HUMIDITY
(Average % humidity at noon)

	JAN	FEB	MAR	APR	MAY	JUN	JUL	AUG	SEP	OCT	NOV	DEC
UK: London	77	72	64	56	57	58	59	62	65	70	78	81
Australia: Sydney	64	65	65	64	63	62	60	56	55	57	60	62
Austria: Salzburg	75	69	61	58	59	59	60	61	53	68	75	79
Bermuda	70	68	68	70	73	75	71	70	71	71	70	70
Canada: Toronto	71	67	62	55	55	55	54	56	59	61	67	71
Canaries: Lanzarote	65	63	59	56	56	59	59	57	59	60	61	63
Cyprus: Nicosia	72	68	67	62	59	56	52	53	57	59	64	70
France: Marseilles	68	60	57	54	54	50	45	49	54	61	66	68
Greece: Athens	62	57	54	48	47	39	34	34	42	52	61	63
Ireland: Dublin	80	76	72	67	69	69	70	72	73	75	79	81
New Zealand: Christchurch	59	60	69	71	69	72	76	66	69	60	64	60
Portugal: Faro	72	70	72	67	67	65	62	63	66	68	70	70
Spain: Alicante	57	56	56	57	57	57	57	58	60	58	57	56
South Africa: Cape Town	52	53	52	55	63	63	63	62	58	55	53	53
Switzerland: Geneva	78	71	62	56	58	58	56	59	65	71	76	79
USA: Miami	59	56	56	56	59	64	64	63	66	64	60	60

SUNSHINE CHART
(Average number of hours of sunshine per month)

	JAN	FEB	MAR	APR	MAY	JUN	JUL	AUG	SEP	OCT	NOV	DEC
UK: London	46	64	113	160	199	213	198	188	142	98	53	40
Australia: Sydney	226	184	195	183	180	189	189	214	216	229	228	229
Austria: Salzburg	71	86	137	159	205	198	209	207	176	137	69	58
Bermuda	151	152	197	227	259	259	301	283	237	196	173	150
Canada: Toronto	77	105	139	170	220	257	287	258	198	154	85	74
Canaries: Lanzarote	202	208	245	259	296	288	301	282	243	236	187	190
Cyprus: Nicosia	180	187	237	264	334	370	389	371	322	277	227	170
France: Marseilles	131	154	191	235	278	306	353	312	247	189	140	118
Greece: Athens	121	146	179	229	277	322	369	358	283	209	144	119
Ireland: Dublin	59	71	104	151	193	180	148	152	118	98	63	49
Italy: Rome	131	124	179	212	263	275	334	301	243	189	123	111
New Zealand: Christchurch	215	182	174	143	133	116	126	145	169	187	206	194
Portugal: Faro	175	195	216	277	318	360	398	361	279	237	182	178
Spain: Alicante	182	192	222	262	307	333	362	331	252	210	180	176
South Africa: Cape Town	340	285	290	232	189	172	199	206	228	266	307	337
Switzerland: Geneva	54	98	169	206	243	269	297	266	199	131	61	44
USA: Miami	239	233	269	283	276	255	270	261	212	200	224	221

Amenities

In the UK even the smallest village can boast a piped water and electricity supply – and often mains sewage and gas as well. However, you cannot count on having all these amenities in some of the more isolated regions of Portugal or on a Greek island, for example.

Shopping is another consideration. If you are thinking of living in a resort, bear in mind that in the off-season the area can be extremely quiet. Many shops and restaurants close for months on end and reopen only when the visitors flock back.

Public transport may be non-existent or infrequent – not only in isolated spots, but in the USA, as well. Telephones may be erratic or hard to get; and qualified tradesmen, such as plumbers and electricians, may be thin on the ground, or much less competent than they claim to be.

Health facilities

The older you become the more you are going to need medical care; this is one of those problems that you can't escape. It is unwise to assume that everywhere you will encounter the same standard of medical care that the British National Health Service provides, though it has to be admitted that in some countries it is considerably better. If you suffer from a serious medical condition which requires constant attention, you should think twice before venturing to out-of-the-way places.

Although reciprocal health arrangements exist between the UK and a number of countries, you may need to make a contribution towards the cost of treatment, particularly if you have not reached pensionable age. In others you may discover that state healthcare is woefully inadequate and you have to fork out for private treatment. In others you may simply not qualify for state health benefits.

Even if the treatment is superb, you may find that you cannot take certain facilities for granted. For instance, not all state health schemes have facilities for convalescence after an illness or cover dental charges. This topic is treated in greater depth in Chapter 5.

Language

Do the locals speak your language or, perhaps, more importantly, do you speak theirs? Problems of communication can occur in popular retirement locations in Europe, particularly when an emergency strikes. If you are rushed to hospital, for instance, how will you cope if none of the staff can speak English?

If you are to make the most of your new surroundings it makes sense to get to grips with the local tongue. You will then be able to bargain for goods in the market, understand national TV programmes, deal with the tradesmen and make friends with the locals.

Some people get by without using the local vernacular; amazingly, an estimated 80 per cent of British settlers in Spain cannot speak a word of Spanish. However, I doubt if you will feel entirely at home in a place unless you understand the language of the majority.

It is a very wise investment to enrol for a course in the language of your adoptive country months or even years before you settle there. You will immediately see the benefit when it comes to negotiating the purchase or rental of a property there. While some interpretation will probably be needed, you will at least be able to grasp what is happening.

Cultural and organisational differences

Apart from language differences there may be differences in temperament and attitude to contend with. Southern Europeans, for instance, often have a more leisurely attitude to life than British people do, and you may get irritated if you have urgent matters to attend to and all activities grind to a stop for the siesta...or an unexpected fiesta.

Customs may be different: you may have to put up with noisy festivals that go on the whole night; the bureaucracy may be pervasive and inefficient – obtaining a telephone line, for instance, may take an age; and there may be all kinds of quirky laws that you need to obey. However, these are often deeply rooted practices and traditions, and a foreigner is powerless to change them. If you try, you are likely to make yourself very unpopular.

Rather than get upset because things are not organised the way they are back home, you need to recognise these differences and make an effort to come to terms with them. This means reading up about the country and its people and ensuring that you are thoroughly briefed before you go.

Taxation

This also deserves investigation. There are places, such as Andorra, which are tax havens, and others where personal taxation is higher than in the UK. Do not assume that you are exempt from taxation in your adopted country. If you have permanent residence status, the chances are that you are not, and you could experience a nasty surprise when the tax authorities finally catch up with you.

Apart from income tax there are other taxes to consider, such as capital gains tax, inheritance tax, local taxes, wealth tax, value added tax or purchase tax. As countries develop their infrastructures, taxes rise, and you cannot count on a country remaining a low-tax or low-cost haven for ever.

Immigration or property restrictions

Do not assume that the world is your oyster. There are countries that place obstacles in the way of any intending retirees from abroad. In the past many Swiss cantons have placed quotas on the number of foreign owners of property in their area. In the United States there is no restriction on property ownership by foreigners, but there is on permanent residence status.

In order to retire to other countries you may well have to meet certain financial requirements so that you do not prove a drain on the country's resources. If you plan to retire to Australia, for instance, you will need to show the authorities that you have a substantial amount of capital.

Member states of the European Union tend to be more liberal towards the nationals of other member states. As a UK citizen you will not need a visa to enter an EU country, and you will be eligible for a residence permit of five years, renewable provided you are covered by sickness insurance and receiving a pension or benefit which is at least higher than the level of the minimum social security pension of the host country.

The basic state pension in the UK tends to be lower than that of virtually every other EU country. This means that UK pensioners may need to demonstrate that they have sufficient additional income in order to qualify for permanent residence in certain countries.

Social life

Some people are naturally gregarious and feel happiest when they are mixing with other people of their own nationality. Others are able to live quite happily with local people without an elaborate expatriate social network to sustain them. Your lifestyle may well determine your retirement location.

The former category will prefer to be in a town, probably with a substantial expatriate community with its own churches, bridge clubs, amateur dramatic societies, etc. The latter can be more adventurous and perhaps opt for a village off the beaten track where they will mix more readily with the locals.

In the country sections of this book I sometimes indicate which areas are popular with British settlers so you will know where to look or where not to look for a property.

Your pension

Although you are entitled to receive your UK state pension in any country of the world where you retire, the amount you receive will vary from country to country. State retirement pensions often represent a major slice of pensioners' incomes, and you will clearly lose out if you settle in a country where your pension is frozen (ie it is not adjusted annually after your departure from the UK). This is not a problem if you are taking up residence in another country of the European Union, but British pensioners settling in Australia, Canada and New Zealand, for instance, miss out financially.

This very important matter is dealt with at greater length in Chapter 5.

Stability and security

Not every country turns out to be a secure retirement haven, and what today may seem a perfectly peaceful place might tomorrow undergo a revolution or change of government. Extreme nationalist governments may resent the presence of foreigners, and history is full of instances of foreign property being confiscated and no compensation offered.

Security is also important. While there are still places on earth where people go out leaving their doors unlocked, they are becoming fewer. In urban areas, particularly, theft can be quite common.

Accessibility to the UK

Most people want to retain contact with the UK, so proximity to an airport and good air connections can be important. Most countries offer direct flights to London's international airports, and some have services to regional airports in the UK, too. The world has become a much smaller place.

The closer you are the more frequent your visits can be. This is one of the attractions of Europe where flights are frequent and never take more than a few hours. Thanks to charter operators and low-cost airlines, air fares to the more popular areas are fairly affordable. You also have the option of travelling by road or rail, now much speedier with the opening of the Channel Tunnel.

Another advantage of being close to the UK is that you are more likely to have visits from friends and relations living in the UK.

Which country?

You probably have a shrewd idea of where you would like to retire to. If the decision is entirely in your hands you will doubtless plump for a country with which you are familiar and where you believe you will feel at ease.

If you have a number of alternatives in mind it would be well worth using this chapter as a checklist to help you decide which one will be best for you. There are pros and cons for each one.

European Union countries on the whole have good health services, are close to the UK and your state pension is adjusted annually, but the cost of living in some of them can be high, and unless you become fluent in the local language there could be communication difficulties. Southern Europe is not so expensive and its resorts attract tens of thousands of pensioners from Northern Europe.

In Australia, Canada and New Zealand the way of life may be familiar and easy to get used to but regular travel between the two countries and the UK can work out prohibitively expensive and your state pension will be frozen. People often move to these countries if they already have friends and relations there but there could be problems in obtaining the requisite residence visa.

The USA is relatively inexpensive compared with many European countries, transatlantic flights are frequent and cheap, and your state pension is uprated regularly, but here too you may experience difficulty in obtaining a permanent residence permit. However, there is no obstacle to having a holiday home there where you stay for six months of the year.

South Africa boasts an excellent climate and is relatively cheap but your state pension will lose value and there are doubts about the long-term stability of the country. On the credit side, thanks to the weakness of the rand, the amount of capital required to qualify for residence is currently very modest. Certain parts of the Caribbean are also worth considering if you wish to bask in a warm climate all the year round.

Further on in this book you will find information on the countries and areas of the world which seem most popular with would-be retirees. There are notable omissions: Scandinavia, South America, Asia, Africa, the South Pacific, Eastern Europe. These areas are most likely to attract retirees who already have close connections with the countries concerned.

This is not to say that UK and other EU nationals do not retire to these places. However, those who do are likely to have spent part of their working lives there or have strong ties with the country concerned, and are therefore less likely to need to turn to this book for advice.

FINDING OUT ABOUT THE LOCATION

Before you commit yourself, it is essential to find out as much as possible about the place of intended residence, the bad aspects as well as the good. Brochures from tourist offices and estate agents provide one half of the picture, but for a more realistic appraisal you need to rely on living conditions reports.

If you are thinking of moving to a member country of the European Union, the European Commission publishes a short guide entitled *Living in Another Country* plus a number of factsheets dealing with such matters as right of residence, driving licences, taxes, etc. These are available from European Commission offices and can also be accessed on the Internet: www.citizens.eu.int.

At your local library or bookshop you will find useful handbooks on living in or buying property in various countries. A selection of them are mentioned in the reference section of this book. For really up-to-date information you should subscribe to specialist newspapers and magazines. Outbound Newspapers, for instance, publishes newspapers for would-be emigrants and visitors to Australia, Canada, New Zealand, South Africa and the USA, and there seem to be several glossy magazines about France and Spain.

However, where feasible, you also need to conduct your own thorough reconnaissance, visiting the place(s) you have in mind in order to find out from local residents how they cope and what kind of snags they come up against. A visit to any British consulate in the area might also be a sensible idea; many consulates are happy to provide advice and useful contacts.

4

Acquiring a Property

Once you have a rough idea of where you would like to live, it is sensible to visit the area at different times of the year. Then you are in a better position to decide whether it is a place for all seasons – an area where you could live all the year round – or essentially a holiday destination.

Another advantage of repeated visits is that you will get an overview of the property market and the local facilities. You will also reach a conclusion as to the type of dwelling you would like – a detached villa, a linked house, an apartment, sheltered accommodation, etc.

Even more importantly you will develop local contacts with local knowledge who could prove useful later on. These might include:

- architects and surveyors
- banks
- the local consul
- builders able to repair an older property for you or build a new one
- estate agents
- insurance brokers with local knowledge
- legal advisers with local knowledge
- medical advisers and hospital administrators
- resident expatriates who know the ropes.

RENTING

There is little point in going though the lengthy process of acquiring a property if you are only planning to live in it for a relatively short time. To purchase a villa only to sell it two years later will probably involve you in a loss unless prices rise dramatically in the intervening period, given the costs of buying and selling.

The alternative is to rent. Privately rented accommodation is much more common on the continent than in the UK, particularly in the cities, and may work out cheaper. If you invest your capital rather than use it to buy a property you may find that your annual investment income is more than sufficient to pay the rent. You might also avoid problems relating to inheritance laws in certain countries.

You also need to be aware that in some countries foreigners are not allowed to own property – in many of the former Communist states of Eastern Europe, for instance. However, in Hungary it is now possible provided you get a permit, but in the Czech Republic you would need to form a company with a local partner to effect a purchase. As some of these countries join the European Union, the regulations may change in favour of foreign ownership, but for the time being you will have to make do with renting.

In resorts and in the more rural areas house purchase tends to be the norm among foreigners planning to take up permanent residence. That is not to say that renting is impossible at resorts. House agents and developers will always prefer to sell you a house, but during periods when the housing market is sluggish they may decide it is better to have tenants for properties rather than leave them empty. You may also be able to negotiate a rental agreement with a British property owner who hopes eventually to sell.

In either case it is essential that a proper rental agreement is drawn up and signed, and it is advisable to take legal advice. In France, for instance, the letting of accommodation (apart from holiday lets) is governed by the Loi Méhaignerie.

Case history

Mr and Mrs L initially decided to settle in Portugal – not on the Algarve but close to Lisbon where they found rented accommodation easily. After two years they moved on to France – to rented accommodation in Perpignan. They stayed there for four years and were then offered the opportunity to buy their house at a considerable discount. Although it was a very tempting offer, they decided to return to the UK to be closer to their children and grandchildren.

Your lease
The lease should contain the following details:

- a full description of the property including an inventory of fixtures and fittings
- the rent payable – including the initial deposit
- service charges
- liability for local taxes
- liability for repairs
- duration of lease and any opt-out clauses
- amount of notice to be given.

During your house search renting a home for a short period – rather than staying in a hotel – serves as a useful introduction to living in a particular area. It is worth bearing in mind that in the off-peak season you may be able to rent a holiday property for up to three months from a package holiday operator at very attractive rates. The magazine *Private Villas* contains an exclusive selection of holiday villas to rent.

BUYING

Most people who retire abroad decide to buy a property. This may appear a very attractive proposition since property prices abroad often seem lower than they are in Britain, and if you are about to sell your UK home you will doubtless feel you have money to burn.

However, one should not count one's chickens before they are hatched. Property purchase is a major undertaking which can cost more than you expect, and the last thing you should do is approach it with your eyes closed.

The Romans had a good phrase for it: caveat emptor (let the buyer beware). Very few of us would think of buying a property in the UK without taking legal advice or having the property surveyed, unless it is a new building and subject to a guarantee. Unfortunately, away from these shores people sometimes throw caution to the winds, and in so doing risk losing a lot of money.

There are stories of people paying cash on the nail to developers who have vanished into thin air with the money, of properties that have been sold to several purchasers, of so-called building land which turns out to be a swamp, of half finished properties where the developers have gone bankrupt. If you want to lose money quickly, there is no better way of doing so than to rush into the purchase of property abroad without taking appropriate advice.

'People leave their brains behind at Gatwick Airport,' was a remark I heard time and again on a visit to Spain. However, I must stress that it is not just the gullible who get ripped off by unscrupulous house agents and developers. The British author of a book on house purchase in Florida lost thousands of pounds on his first attempt to buy a house in the United States. If a writer on consumer affairs can get things so wrong, what hope is there for ordinary mortals? I repeat: 'Caveat emptor'.

Old wives' tales
Let me first dispel a few erroneous notions.

'Buying a house abroad is a piece of cake'
This is a matter of opinion: house purchase is always a good deal more complicated than buying a lawnmower wherever you decide to settle down. You may know British conveyancing practices from back to front but elsewhere the procedures may be quite different. This is particularly so on the Continent, and to avoid disaster, you need to know precisely what you are doing. For some countries, notably France and Spain, there are several good books available which go into the intricacies of buying a home, and they deserve your attention.

WHAT YOU NEED TO KNOW BEFORE PROCEEDING

When you are buying a property, especially a new property, you need to satisfy yourself on the following points.

- Am I paying a fair price? Often foreign purchasers are charged over the odds, so you need to compare the price you are quoted with those for similar properties.

- Who is the actual vendor? The builder? A management company? A finance company? The present occupant?

- Is the developer/builder a reputable company with a sound financial base? If in doubt, you could always ask for a reference from his bank.

- Has permission been obtained to build on this site? You may need to check with the local authority.

- Are any more dwellings planned for the site which will obstruct the view? Resort developments are often completed in phases.

- Are there any restrictions on letting the property? Local authorities (eg in Florida) and mortgage lenders sometimes impose restrictions.

- When is the completion date and how soon after can I move in? You also need to check whether all amenities (eg access roads, landscaping) will be ready at this time.

- How safe is my deposit if the project does not go ahead? Ideally the money should be kept by the notary/solicitor/ estate agent in a separate account. However, if you back out of the deal you may forfeit the deposit.

- How experienced and reputable is the management company (in the case of sheltered accommodation, resort developments, apartment blocks)?

- What maintenance and service charges are there likely to be? You should get a quote.

- What charges and taxes are there on top of the purchase price? These would include legal fees and VAT.

- Does the builder offer any guarantee against building defects, and if so, how long is it valid?

- Are there any mortgage schemes available? Some of the larger developers have made special arrangements with their banks.

- What equipment will the home contain? Some can be provided fully furnished (see later on in this chapter).

'House surveys are a waste of time'
The estate agent may tell you this, but it is, after all, in his interest to sell the property as quickly as possible and with the minimum of hassle. Unless the building is new and the house-builder offers guarantees for a specified period, you are strongly advised to have the house surveyed before you sign anything, if only for your own peace of mind.

'DIY conveyancing works out much cheaper'
A minority of people in Britain handle all aspects of the house purchase themselves without the assistance of a solicitor or conveyancing professional. If you try to do this abroad, you could run into serious problems, and may eventually have to employ a lawyer to clear up the mess. Besides, in many countries the involvement of public notaries is obligatory to complete a house purchase.

During the course of my research I came across one person who had looked after the legal side of a house purchase in Spain without incurring any problems. 'I read all the books I could find about buying a house in Spain,' Mr D told me. 'Fortunately I was buying from someone I knew well and whom I could trust. He provided me with all the bills and other documentation to show there were no debts on the house and I was able to deal with the local authority and the notary. However, these were exceptional circumstances, and I would not normally have proceeded in this way.'

'Estate agents are unnecessary'
Buying through an agent will usually cost more than buying direct from the owner, but a good house agent who can help you find the right property abroad and steer you through an unfamiliar buying process is usually worth his commission. Some are even able to arrange mortgage finance and insurance and make arrangements with solicitors. However, it is entirely up to you whether you decide to avail yourself of any of these services.

Established agencies have built up a reputation for integrity and the last thing they want is a dissatisfied customer. On the other hand there are 'cowboys' around who will do anything to clinch a deal and then waltz off with your deposit. You can avoid these by checking if the agent is licensed or a member of a professional body. A select list of agents is provided at the end of this book in Appendix C.

'British solicitors are an expensive luxury'
British lawyers are strictly regulated and have indemnity insurance to compensate their clients for any mistakes. They also speak your language and can therefore explain what you are letting yourself in for in plain English, which is valuable in itself.

However, only a small number of law firms in Britain have expertise in legal procedures in other countries, although they may be able to put you in touch with someone who does. You therefore need to find either:

- a British solicitor with knowledge of the area where you plan to settle and who either has a licence to do conveyancing and other legal work in the country in question or is associated with a firm that does; or

- a local lawyer (or notary in some countries) who has experience of doing conveyancing for British buyers and can explain the conveyancing procedures clearly. You should always check the lawyer's credentials; the nearest British consulate should be able to help.

Whether you choose to engage a British solicitor or his foreign counterpart I would advise against engaging a solicitor (advocate, notary or attorney) who also acts for the vendor, developer or estate agent, because of the danger of conflict of interest. It may cost a little more to employ a solicitor you can trust, but getting good advice right from the outset might spare you a good deal of expense later on.

To be absolutely sure that you are properly covered if the transaction goes badly awry, you might consider taking out title insurance, which would sort out any legal difficulties on your behalf.

If you want to read up about property purchase abroad, you can find books about it in public libraries and bookshops. The Federation of Overseas Property Developers, Agents and Consultants (FOPDAC) and certain law and accountancy firms publish leaflets on the legal aspects of house purchase. Overseas property journals and newspapers often publish up-to-the-minute articles on house purchase abroad, and it could be worthwhile taking out a subscription (see bibliography in Appendix D). There may also be organisations which can offer you advice, such as the Institute of Foreign Property Owners in the case of Spain.

Finding a property

There seems to be no lack of information on overseas property these days, particularly for the more popular countries such as France, Portugal, Spain and the USA (Florida). You can find out about overseas properties from:

- *National newspapers in the UK.* Most of these have a regular section devoted to residential property with editorial and advertisements, and increasingly overseas property is being featured.

- *Specialist magazines and newspapers.* There are a number of UK publications devoted to overseas property, such as *World of Property* and *International Homes*, some of them specialising in a particular country, notably France or Spain. Publications such as *Dalton's Weekly* and *Exchange and Mart* also carry advertisements for homes abroad. (See the bibliography in Appendix D and under individual country entries in Appendix A and Appendix B.)

- *UK estate agents.* A number of estate agents in the UK specialise in selling overseas property and advertise regularly in the publications mentioned above. They represent foreign estate agents, builders and developers or house-owners who wish to sell their properties. Most tend to specialise in one or two countries or a particular region within a country and some publish regular property bulletins. Some belong to a trade association, notably the Federation of Overseas Property Developers, Agents and Consultants (FOPDAC) and the National Association of Estate Agents (NAEA).

- *Developers.* Some developers handle their own marketing, particularly the British ones. Others prefer to use an estate agent as an intermediary.

- *Overseas property exhibitions and seminars.* Exhibitions and seminars are held at different locations round the country. Some are small-scale affairs in which just one estate agent or developer displays his wares, but there are larger events organised by FOPDAC and property magazines where any number of agents, developers, financial advisers, lawyers and removals specialists exhibit.

- *Foreign newspapers and magazines.* If you have friends or relations living in the area where you hope to settle you could ask if they can either forward property advertisements from local papers or suggest a publication dealing with property to which you could subscribe. Newspapers circulating among the expatriate community often contain advertisements for properties.

- *Foreign estate agents.* Many estate agents abroad that have a foreign clientele advertise in the publications mentioned above and may also participate in overseas property exhibitions. Some are represented by agents in the UK. (See Appendix C.)

- *By word of mouth.* You may have relatives or friends who have settled abroad who know of properties for sale. The grapevine is surprisingly effective, and researchers from the University of Surrey found the majority of people moving to Spain had found their retirement home this way.

Beware of people who approach you out of the blue when you are on holiday offering to sell you a house. Even if the offer seems a good one, you should proceed with extreme caution and not sign any agreement until you have taken legal advice.

Inspection tours

It is absolutely essential to see before you buy, and this means a visit to the properties in which you are interested.

There are two types of inspection tour: the type which is organised for you and the type you organise yourself.

Organised inspection tours

These are short visits – typically of three days' duration – organised by a developer or estate agents, which enable you to view a number of properties in a particular area over a short time. The cost of the trip which usually includes hotel accommodation is often subsidised: £50 trips to Spain are not uncommon.

Trips of this nature have advantages – they are inexpensive and you are escorted to the properties that are up for sale – but they have a few drawbacks:

- you may only see the properties that the developer or estate agent has on offer;

- you may find yourself under pressure (or else feel obliged) to put down a deposit on a property even if you are not entirely happy with it;

- the marketing costs – notably, the subsidised inspection trips – add to the final price of the property;

- a few days are insufficient for you to decide whether you could settle down happily in the area or not;

- in many cases the agents/developers are interested in selling new properties – not secondhand ones.

Independent inspection visits

The principle of an inspection visit is a good one, but you may well find it more satisfactory to organise your own visit in your own time and at your own expense. A travel agent can usually organise a cheap flight, hotel accommodation and car hire. If you contact some overseas property agents before you go they will offer you brochures, contact addresses and maps.

This is a more expensive way of doing things, of course, but it has the advantage that there will be no pressure on you or sense of obligation to sign a contract. You also have a chance to view a wider selection of properties – including ones that are not being sold through an agent.

I stress the importance of viewing a number of properties rather than taking the first one you set eyes on. Even if you return to your first choice the exercise will not be in vain, for you will be able to compare it with other available property in the area in terms of quality and price – useful ammunition to have in your armoury when negotiations start.

There can come a time, however, when one property starts to look very like another. You therefore need to make notes on each property either as you go round or immediately after completing your visit.

CHECKLIST

- *Layout*: the best idea is to make a rough plan of the dwelling with approximate dimensions.

- *Rooms*: are there enough of them? (You may want to accommodate visitors.) Are they the right size?

- *Bathroom*: you need to investigate the plumbing and the water heating system. Some modern developments have solar panels on the roof.

- *Kitchen*: find out what equipment, if any, comes with the kitchen (eg cooker, cupboard space, kitchen sink unit).

- *Utilities*: is the house supplied with mains electricity, gas, water? Is it connected to the mains sewer? Is there a telephone? If not, what are the connection charges?

- *Heating and ventilation*: check whether there are fans and/or air conditioning and – since in some places it can get chilly in winter – heating arrangements.

- *Garden* (if applicable): note its size and try to assess how difficult it will be to maintain. If it is large, it would be sensible to check on the availability of gardeners.

- *Position*: enquire how far away the nearest shops are, and also the nearest public transport routes.

- *Miscellaneous*: number and position of power points, height of working surfaces, stairs (can you get up and down them easily?), light fittings, security, view.

Buying a new property

A house which has been built recently will be much easier to maintain than an older one and, if brand new, will often carry a guarantee – though this may be of very limited duration. Also building standards are now being controlled more rigorously in countries such as Spain and Portugal, so the possibility of the structure falling down if you slam the front door is now very remote.

As in the UK marketing of new properties starts as they are being built. One advantage of putting down a deposit on a new property before it is completed is that you may be able to have modifications incorporated in the design, such as your own colour scheme. However, it is not advisable to buy purely on the strength of what you have read in a brochure: you actually need to go and see a show home or examples of past work by the builder before you sign any agreement or part with any cash.

Generally speaking, a new home will be more cost-effective to run, with no major repairs or decoration necessary for several years, and if you need to raise finance for its purchase the developer may be able to come up with a mortgage scheme.

Yet one should proceed with caution. There have been innumerable instances of developers – particularly in Florida and Southern Europe – going out of business leaving houses half finished, and of money changing hands and developers disappearing into thin air. Caveat emptor – as I said before. Make sure that the company you are dealing with is reliable and trustworthy.

If the property includes a garden you will need to find out if any landscaping is to be done. Knocking it into shape yourself can be a back-breaking task. For this reason some people prefer to live in apartment blocks or on managed estates with communal gardens and – in warm climates and resorts – a swimming pool.

However, such arrangements can have their drawbacks. In most cases a substantial service charge is payable on a monthly basis to cover such items as maintenance of the structure, decoration and cleaning of communal areas, maintenance of the lift(s), porterage, the upkeep of the garden and swimming pool, lighting of communal areas and security. Furthermore, such charges have a nasty habit of rising every year.

Buying second-hand

Amongst younger retirees there is considerable interest in older properties. In certain countries, notably France and Italy, secondhand properties can often be bought quite cheaply in areas remote from the main conurbations. However, you may well have to spend a considerable amount of money modernising them.

The more adventurous may follow the tradition we have in Britain of buying redundant farm buildings for conversion into homes, though it is essential to obtain planning permission before making the purchase. It is worth remarking that conversion and refurbishment do not come cheap and there is a risk that you will not recoup your costs if you have to sell up. You may also encounter problems in raising a loan on the property.

The less intrepid will probably be happier with a property built during the past few decades with a mature garden and closer to an urban centre. You need to bear in mind that as you grow older and less agile, comfort and convenience will count for more than looks. If you do not have your own car, you will need to be close to public transport routes.

Even if the property seems sound enough, it is advisable to have it inspected by a surveyor or architect. Attention needs to be paid to the following:

- *Walls and ceilings* – look out for cracks, signs of damp, discoloration, bulges.

- *Floors and woodwork* – look for evidence of dry rot or infestation.

- *Roof* – look out for signs of sagging or missing tiles and inspect the guttering.

- *Windows* – look for signs of rot or leaking and make sure they open and shut easily.

- *Plumbing and wiring* – you need to investigate these thoroughly to see if they need renewal. The electricity supplier may insist on rewiring before it is prepared to connect you to the mains.

- *Alterations* – find out if the property has been altered in any way and, if so, how well this has been done.

Having a house built

Another option is to buy a plot of land and build your own home. This is more expensive than buying a dwelling on an established development and there are several pitfalls. You should not assume, for instance, that because a plot of land is up for sale that it is possible to build on it. In Spain, for instance, a distinction is drawn between *finca urbana* (land earmarked for construction) and *finca rustica* (agricultural land) and it is much more difficult to obtain planning permission to build on the latter. Don't take the vendor's world for it, but check with the local authorities before money changes hands.

You will need to engage the services of

- a lawyer to handle the legal intricacies
- an architect to draw up plans and supervise the construction
- a builder.

In some countries you may have to engage additional help.

In Spain it is customary to employ an *aparejador*, a kind of building surveyor.

Among the matters that have to be checked are:

- whether the property can be connected up easily to the necessary services (such as electricity, water and drainage) and, if so, the likely cost;

- whether there is proper access to your property for vehicles;

- whether there are any planning applications on neighbouring land which could lead to undesirable developments;

- whether the local authority has any plans (eg road widening or a motorway) that might affect the site;

- whether there are restrictions on the type of dwelling to be put on the site (eg size, materials).

Retirement accommodation

Older people may value their independence, but they do not all want to soldier on alone, particularly if their health is failing. That is why the past decade has seen an increase in sheltered housing schemes in the UK. These provide independent living units as well as communal facilities for residents and there is normally a warden or house manager to oversee arrangements.

Provision for retirees is well advanced in the USA where in the sunnier states, such as Arizona and Florida, you will find retirement villages and towns with a full range of medical, transport and recreational facilities for the elderly. Leisure World, for instance, boasts some 15,000 residents.

In many countries of continental Europe sheltered housing is less common, since the elderly have traditionally been looked after by their families.

However, the position is changing, and during the course of my research for this book I came across two developments on the Côte d'Azur in France and three on the Costa Blanca in Spain but built with expatriates in mind. One of the latter has a nursing home (*residencia*) attached for residents who need constant medical supervision.

Such housing arrangements are specially designed to meet the needs of people as they grow older and often feature mid-level switches and points, assistance rails in bathrooms, an alarm system with transmitters worn on the body and doctor's surgeries held in the premises.

Purchasing arrangements differ. Here are three kinds of contract that I came across in Spain:

- you buy the residential unit outright and can sell it on to another person at the prevailing market rate;

- you purchase the leasehold of a unit for a fixed term (eg 20 years) at the end of which it reverts to the landlord. You are able to sell on the unexpired part of the lease either to the landlord or a third party;

- you purchase the leasehold of the unit for life. When you die or move out it reverts to the landlord.

Inevitably there is an annual service charge, which is likely to rise year by year, and you may be liable for local taxes. Since such complexes are often more elaborate than sheltered housing schemes in the UK (all the ones I saw had a swimming pool and other outdoor recreational facilities), the charges inevitably work out more expensive.

Some of the sheltered housing schemes I visited on the Continent are run on similar lines to those operated in Britain by companies like McCarthy and Stone and Westbury Retirement Homes, the main difference being that they cater for people of all nationalities and have regular doctor's surgeries on the premises.

They are ideal for people who appreciate having a certain amount of independence but also like to be insulated from some of the problems connected with living abroad. It would be sensible to visit a few sheltered housing schemes in the UK first, to decide whether you fall into this category and therefore whether sheltered housing in the sun is an option you wish to explore.

Buying a furniture and household equipment package
If you decide that it is impracticable to ship out your own
furniture to your new residence and do not relish the
prospect of having to furnish it from scratch, you may be
able to arrange for the place to be furnished for you.

In the USA, for instance, developers can offer fully
furnished and equipped homes, and resort management
companies in southern Europe can offer a similar service.
Alternatively you could ask your estate agent or a wholesale
furniture store to carry out the job for you – providing you
with everything from a bed to a bottle-opener.

LEGAL ASPECTS OF BUYING A PROPERTY

Once you are certain that you have found the right place,
you can commence the purchasing process. If you are buying
through a reputable house agent or developer they should
explain the procedures you will need to go through or put
you in touch with the professionals who will.

In some countries the system is radically different from
that in England and Wales, and you need to understand
what is happening; Scottish buyers, however, will find
continental practices more familiar.

It would seem obvious to vest the ownership of the
property in your own name or in joint names (eg yourself
and your partner). However, given the different tax regimes
and inheritance laws on the Continent, in particular, you
might find it beneficial to explore other options, such as
buying the property in the name of your children or
designated heirs or registering it in the name of a limited
company. An experienced lawyer or accountant should be
able to advise you.

Players in the game
In continental Europe, for instance, you may have difficulty
in discovering who does what. Here is a breakdown of the
players in the conveyancing game.

TYPICAL HOUSE INVENTORY

Kitchen
Table, chairs, cooker, washing machine, sink, draining board, refrigerator.
Bread bin, breadboard/chopping board, kettle, oven cloth, table cloth, tray, washing-up bowl with brush or sponge, biscuit/cake tin, butter dish, cake plate, condiment set, mixing bowl, milk jug, one-pint measuring jug, sugar basin, teapot, toast rack, water jug, cutlery box or divided drawer, breadknife, carving knife, fork and dish, corkscrew and bottle opener, fish slice, grater, kitchen scissors, ladle, potato peeler, potato masher, rolling pin, sharp vegetable knife, tea strainer, tin opener, whisk, wooden spoon, baking tin, casserole dish and lid, colander, frying pan, saucepans (large, medium, small), oven roasting tray, pie dish.

Living room
Lounge suite, coffee table, standard lamps, cocktail cabinet, TV set, video-recorder, radio, compact disc player.

Dining room
Table, chairs, dresser.
At least four of each: knife, fork (table and dessert), spoon (tea, soup, dessert), plate (large, medium, small), tea cup and saucer and mug, cereal/soup/dessert bowl, tumbler, wine glass, egg cup, table spoon, place mat. Tea and dinner service must each be of matching patterns.

Bedroom
Bed(s), lamps, dressing table, wardrobe(s), clock radio.
Per bed:
Two sheets/fitted sheets, one under blanket, two blankets and a bedspread, or one continental quilt (and cover), two pillows per person, two pillow cases.

Bathroom
Washbasin, toilet, shower (with shower curtain), bath.
Bathmat, toilet roll holder, waste-bin, bathroom cabinet with mirror.

General
Broom, bucket, cleaning agents, clothes pegs, door mat, duster, dustpan and brush, floor cloth, spare light bulbs, vacuum cleaner.

The notary
The role of the notary differs from country to country. In France, for example, a notary is a public official who generally draws up and witnesses the final contract. Since he has to give impartial advice to vendor and purchaser he is traditionally employed by both parties in the transaction. Nevertheless, it is advisable to appoint your own notary in order to obtain practical advice.

In Spain and several other European countries the notary certifies that the contract is prepared, signed and authenticated in accordance with the law and does not normally offer practical advice.

The counselling lawyer
You are strongly advised to obtain legal advice from a counselling lawyer – *abogado* (Spain), *advogado* or *solicitador* (Portugal), *avvocato* (Italy), *Rechtsanwalt* or *Avocat* (Austria and Switzerland) – who is not acting on behalf of the vendors. There are a number of solicitors in the UK who can undertake this on your behalf or who can instruct a lawyer licensed to practise in the country in question. The lawyer will conduct searches for you and negotiate the terms of the contract with the vendor.

The translator
Unless you are proficient in the language of the country you should also have all the legal documents translated into English. In some countries you have to employ a translator who is licensed to deal with legal documents.

The estate agent
Many people buy properties through estate agents, either in the country concerned or based in the UK. British agents represent developers, vendors and often foreign estate agents, and have local representatives to show you properties and steer you through the buying procedures.

A number of countries in Europe and elsewhere have a state licensing system for estate agents and penalise those who do not comply with a strict code of practice. When abroad, you should steer clear of people who claim to be estate agents but turn out not to be, since if something goes wrong you will have no legal redress.

Many of the British firms are members of the Federation of Overseas Property Developers, Agents and Consultants, the National Association of Estate Agents or a similar professional body, and members are expected to abide by a strict code of conduct.

It is worth noting that in several European countries it is the practice for the purchaser, not the vendor, to pay the estate agent's commission. You should enquire about this from the outset.

The surveyor or architect
If you are purchasing an older property it is advisable to have a structural survey done, whatever the house agent or your legal advisers say. This need not be a national of the country concerned; in fact, some purchasers ask a UK-based surveyor to inspect the dwelling for them despite the additional cost.

The mortgage lender
If you need to raise a mortgage in order to purchase a property, you will find that a number of British-based building societies, mortgage brokers and banks offer home loans for properties in the European Union – sometimes though an overseas subsidiary. Developers, estate agents and solicitors may be able to arrange a financial package for you, but it is always a good idea to ask around.

The buying process
- Choose the property (and have it surveyed, if necessary).

- Arrange for the transfer of money. If you do not wish to pay a lump sum you will need to arrange a mortgage. Keep evidence of any money transfers, as you may need to produce them should you eventually decide to sell and want to export the proceeds.

- Sign a purchase agreement. This is a preliminary contract which is a legally binding contract to buy on the terms stated. (The contract will usually include a detailed description of the property which needs to be checked carefully.)

- Pay a deposit. On the European continent this could be 10–15% of the price of the property. It is essential to note that this is non-refundable if you decide to back out of the deal. Ideally the deposit should be lodged with the notary – not the vendor – and kept in a separate account.

- Carry out the usual planning and title searches. Normally your counselling lawyer (or the notary) will do this for you, but you need to check that this is being done in accordance with your wishes. The work involves:
  - checking that the vendor is the registered owner of the property and has the right to sell it;
  - checking that there are no mortgages or other charges registered on the property;
  - checking that planning consents have been obtained and building regulations complied with;
  - finding out about future plans for development in the area and on adjacent properties;
  - checking that the vendor is up to date in payment of municipal taxes and other charges (eg service charges). (Receipts should be produced and checked.)

- Have a draft ownership transfer agreement drawn up if the search is satisfactory. (This should be re-checked against the property.)

- Sign the agreement. This may have to be done in the presence of a notary.

- Pay the balance. (Make sure you get a receipt for the correct amount.)

- Register the agreement with the land registry – or check that this is being done.

- Insure the property.

HOW MUCH WILL IT COST?

The following list should help you to calculate the total cost of buying a new home abroad. Not all the items will be applicable.

Price of property (including fixtures and fittings)   _____

Conveyancing fees (notary or solicitor)   _____

Additional legal fees   _____

Survey   _____

VAT or transfer tax   _____

Land registry fees   _____

Estate agent's commission   _____

Interpreter   _____

Translation of documents   _____

Stamp duty (on purchase or mortgage deed)   _____

Money transfer fees   _____

Mortgage arrangement fees   _____

Removal costs   _____

Travel costs   _____

Connection charges (telephone, water, electricity, etc)   _____

Insurance   _____

VAT   _____

Even if you take the best legal advice it is just possible that your title to the whole or part of the property is flawed in some way which might even lead to your losing possession of it. There could, for instance, be acts of fraud adversely affecting your title, the notary may have made mistakes, or you may find there is a boundary dispute, a lack of access or a right of way going right through your property. If you prefer to err on the side of caution, you might consider taking out title insurance which would either solve the problem or make good any loss you may incur.

This chapter can do little more than provide an overview of the ins and outs of house purchase. There are a number of books which provide details on practice in specific countries and they are mentioned in the country sections (Appendix A and Appendix B).

5

Health and Social Security

Two topics are of particular importance to people retiring abroad: their pension (even if they have not reached retirement age) and healthcare provision. Even if you still feel young at heart, you need to face the fact that your health is likely to decline with age and you will become more dependent on the services available.

An increasing number of people are members of private pension schemes or have taken out private health insurance. However, few of us can afford to ignore any state benefits to which we are entitled, and this chapter deals principally with these.

The UK has concluded a number of social security agreements with other countries including members of the European Economic Area – Austria, Belgium, Denmark, Finland, France, Greece, Iceland, Italy, Liechtenstein, Luxembourg, the Netherlands, Norway, Portugal, Ireland, Spain and Sweden. You should note that the EEA is likely to have more members in due course as more countries join the European Union.

The other countries with which the UK has an agreement are Barbados, Bermuda, Canada, Cyprus, Israel, Jamaica, Jersey and Guernsey, Malta, Mauritius, New Zealand, the Philippines, Switzerland, Turkey, the USA and the republics of the former Yugoslavia (such as Bosnia, Croatia, Slovenia, Macedonia).

More agreements of this nature could be signed in the future, so if the country you are retiring to is not in the above lists you should consult with the Benefits Agency. Since the treaties differ to a greater or lesser degree (not all include provision for free medical treatment, for instance), you ought to obtain a copy of the relevant leaflet from the

Agency outlining the benefits for which you are eligible and how to claim them. If your local office does not have the relevant leaflets, you can contact the Overseas Branch in Newcastle.

YOUR STATE PENSION

If you are of pensionable age or in receipt of a widow's or invalidity pension you will need to inform the Pensions Service and discuss arrangements for the payment of your pension when you are abroad. If your local social security office is not able to advise you or supply you with the necessary forms for completion, you should contact the Pensions Service's Overseas Branch giving your full name, date of birth and, where possible, your National Insurance or pension number. The address is in Appendix C.

If you live in Northern Ireland you should direct your enquiries to the Social Security Agency (Overseas Branch).

You can choose various methods of payment:

- by credit transfer to your bank or building society in the UK. If you are planning to stay abroad for only part of the year, this may be the best plan, since you will not need to change payment arrangements when you move;

- by credit transfer to an overseas bank or institution where such a facility is available;

- by a sterling payment cheque to you, your overseas bank or an agent nominated by you every four or 13 weeks;

- in a lump sum on your return (if you are away for no more than two years).

At the time of writing special arrangements need to be made if you are going to certain countries.

Applying for a pension when abroad
If you reach retirement age after you have moved abroad you will normally receive a letter from the Pensions Service

Currently (2002) UK state retirement pensions are paid at the rate prevailing in the UK in the following countries:

Alderney, Austria, Barbados, Belgium, Bermuda, Cyprus, Denmark, Finland, France, Germany, Gibraltar, Greece, Guernsey, Iceland, Ireland, Israel, Isle of Man, Italy, Jamaica, Jersey, Luxembourg, Malta, Mauritius, Norway, Netherlands, Philippines, Portugal, Sark, Spain, Sweden, Switzerland, Turkey, USA, former states of Yugoslavaia (Bosnia, Croatia, Macedonia, Slovenia, etc).

If you are planning to live in a country not featured on this list you should assume that your pension will be frozen at the level at which it stands when you leave.

inviting you to claim a UK retirement pension, provided you have kept the Agency posted about any changes of address. If you do not receive a letter around four months before your 60th birthday (in the case of a woman) or your 65th (in the case of a man) you should contact the Agency.

If you reside in any European Union country you may make a pension claim direct to your country of residence rather than to the one in which you have been insured. The country in which you live will then pass on the details of your claim to the Pensions Service.

If you have made social insurance contributions to more than one country in the European Union (as well as certain other countries), your pension will be made up of pro rata contributions from the UK and the country of residence.

The following procedure would be used in calculating pension entitlement:

- Each country works out the amount of pension payable on the basis of insurance under its own social security scheme only.

- Your social security records are combined and each country works out what would be payable if your social

security contributions had been paid into its own social
security scheme.

• You are informed by each country which of the two
  calculations produces the highest rate of pension, and
  this will be paid to you automatically.

Uprated and frozen pensions

In the UK retirement pensions are adjusted annually to
reflect any change in the retail price index, and for as long
as I can remember because of inflation this has meant an
annual rise for pensioners. Once you leave Britain to take
up residence elsewhere, you cannot count on this regular
uprating.

In about thirty countries, including the USA and much
of Europe, you receive the same amount of pension as
pensioners still resident in the UK. Not that you will
necessarily feel richer if your pension is uprated: if sterling
weakens against the currency of the country you are living
in, you could find your pension buys you less.

Unfortunately, if you retire elsewhere you may well find
your state pension is frozen. That means it stays at the rate
prevailing when you leave Britain or become entitled to a
pension (whichever occurs later). Thus some people who
retired abroad in 1961 are receiving a state pension of under
£3, and those who retired in 1980 are drawing less than £30.

This is an important consideration if you are thinking of
retiring to Australia, Canada, New Zealand or South
Africa, for example, where your state pension is not
uprated. The Caribbean is something of a puzzle: if you
retire to Barbados or Jamaica, your pension will be
increased annually; in Trinidad it remains frozen. It is worth
bearing in mind that there are currently over 490,000 British
expatriates with frozen state pensions.

There are a number of expatriates' pressure groups at
home and abroad campaigning for a change in the law,
notably the Canadian Alliance of British Pensioners and the
British Australian Pensioners' Association. While it is
always possible that the government will have a change of

heart some time in the future, you cannot bank on it. Hence you need to check whether your pension will be frozen or not if you decide to retire to a particular country.

Finally, let us end on a more cheerful note. If you return to the UK, even for a short holiday, your pension will be paid at the prevailing rate, provided you inform the Overseas Branch of the Pensions Service. War pensions and war widows' pensions are not frozen.

OTHER PENSIONS

The majority of people retiring abroad will also receive pensions from the companies or organisations for which they have worked in the past. Self-employed people are usually in private pension schemes.

If you have worked in the public sector your pension will be index-linked in line with inflation. Most company pension plans aim to increase their payouts in a similar manner. Private pension plans vary, and one should beware of plans offering a fixed income which does not rise in value.

In Chapter 6 I caution people not to rely on pensions alone when they retire abroad. In the past people have retired to places where the cost of living has increased more rapidly than the value of their pension. It is therefore vital to have reserves that you can drawn on if such a situation arises.

If you have a personal pension you should review your pension arrangements before it becomes due and before you go abroad to ensure that tax liability is minimised and that the income generated will be sufficient for your needs.

ADDITIONAL STATE BENEFITS

If you are going to live abroad permanently you will no longer be eligible for certain benefits, such as disability living allowance, attendance allowance or income support.

However, over-60s receiving Winter Fuel Allowance

before leaving the UK will normally continue to be eligible for it if they move to any EEA country and Switzerland.

If you make enquiries, you may discover you are eligible for other benefits available to nationals of your country of residence, such as cheap travel. The European Commission has proposed an EU Over-Sixties Card which would offer concessions on public transport and to cultural activities.

You should not assume that every country has the same range of benefits as are available in the UK. For example, if your savings fall below a certain level in Britain, you can claim a number of supplementary benefits, but few other countries have welfare systems that are quite so generous in this respect. The Overseas Branch of the Benefits Agency will be able to advise you.

HEALTH SERVICE

Sad to relate, the older you become the greater the likelihood that you will need medical treatment. It is therefore essential to investigate the health provision in the country and the area of the country where you are planning to settle, and find out if you are eligible for it. The Department of Health Overseas Branch should be able to advise you, otherwise you could enquire at the embassy or consulate of the country concerned.

In some countries you will be eligible for free treatment for most conditions; in others only very basic care is provided free, and you will need to take out private health insurance to supplement the basic treatment. In others you have no option but to take out private insurance.

Items that you may well have to pay for in part or in full include:

- dental treatment
- prescribed medicines

- ambulance travel
- optician's charges
- home nursing.

As far as European Union countries are concerned if you are receiving a state invalidity or retirement pension or widow's benefit from the UK you and your dependents will normally be entitled to the health services of the sickness insurance organisation of an EU country. To prove your eligibility you need to obtain Form E121 from your local social security office before you go. This is not to be confused with Form E111 which is for holidays and business trips only.

If you are not in receipt of any benefit or pension you may be entitled to medical treatment under the health insurance scheme of a European Union country. However, you will normally be required to produce evidence that you have contributed to the UK National Insurance scheme for a certain period. The National Insurance Contributions Office (International Services) can provide you with the necessary certificate.

If you have not reached pensionable age, you will probably be expected to join the insurance scheme in the country of settlement or else take out private health insurance.

Private health insurance

If you find that there are gaps in the public healthcare provision of the country you are planning to retire to or that you are not eligible for all the healthcare benefits you should seriously consider taking out a private health insurance plan.

You may already subscribe to such a scheme, in which case it would be worthwhile enquiring whether it could be extended to cover residence abroad: BUPA, Exeter Friendly Society and PPP are among the insurance companies which offer international plans. Most plans specify an upper age limit for joining – typically 65 or 75 – and insurance cover for the US and Canada will work out more expensive than for the rest of the world because of the high cost of health treatment in North America.

Alternatively you may decide to take out private health insurance in your country of residence, which often works out cheaper. The reason for this is that the insurance company or brokerage sometimes has its own clinics and hospitals or can negotiate special terms for its patients.

You should check whether the following are included in the policy. If not, a supplement may be payable:

- dental care
- spectacles and contact lenses
- medical evacuation (to UK or a centre of medical excellence)
- prescribed medicines
- visits to other countries
- home nursing
- psychiatric treatment
- osteopathy, homeopathy or chiropractic treatment
- physiotherapy.

You also need to ask:

- Are there exclusions (eg if I take part in certain sports)?
- Are there any illnesses not covered?
- Do costs increase after I reach a certain age?
- Do I become eligible immediately on joining or is there a waiting period?
- Is there a ceiling on my medical cover, and what happens if my treatment exceeds this?

If you have difficulty in choosing a plan, you could contact Healthsearch, an organisation which provides impartial advice on medical insurance plans for a small fee. Healthsearch operates a postal service and can also arrange face-to-face consultations. After you have completed the Healthsearch questionnaire you are sent a search analysis report recommending the two plans which best suit your circumstances.

Eligibility for medical treatment on visits to the UK

If you are resident in another country you will be expected to make use of the medical scheme in that country. Should you decide to return to the UK expressly for medical treatment you may well find that you are not eligible for free treatment under the NHS since you are no longer a UK resident. The only exception is if the medical authorities of the country in question refer you to the UK for treatment. This sometimes happens in the case of Gibraltar, for instance. Where there is a social security agreement in place between the UK and the country where you normally reside, you may be entitled to *emergency* medical treatment if you fall ill during your visit. However, you should check the details of the agreement first of all, and if there is any doubt, you should take out private insurance for your trip.

Keeping healthy

To avoid spending one's retirement hanging around doctors' surgeries or in hospital it makes sense to keep yourself as fit as possible. While it is not possible to ward off every illness, a sensible lifestyle can do a great deal to keep you in trim.

Regular exercise

If you have opted for retirement in the sun there will be plenty of open air attractions, including golf, swimming, tennis, bowls (or the local equivalent). Strenuous exercise is best avoided: jogging, squash, football and rugby, for instance can lead to heart attacks or injuries, unless you are exceptionally fit.

Social activity

Even if you are a shy retiring type it is essential to get out and meet people. Introspection is fine in small doses, but shutting yourself off from other people may turn you into a misery and you will start to imagine you are seriously ill.

Sensible food

A well balanced diet is important with plenty of fresh fruit, vegetables and protein. Sugar and fatty foods should be avoided as much as possible: fry-ups and cream cakes should not form part of your regular diet.

Alcohol in moderation
Alcohol can be beneficial if taken in moderate quantities; it helps you to relax. However, the availability of cheap wines and spirits, particularly in southern Europe, can lead to excessive consumption, and this in turn can cause cirrhosis of the liver, degeneration of the arteries, the shakes, etc.

No smoking
Smoking is a killer. It causes lung cancer, chest infections and coronary disease – hardly the ideal accompaniment to your retirement lifestyle. If you can't kick the habit, graduate to cigars or a pipe.

Prevention
Operate on the principle that prevention is better than cure. Take the necessary vaccinations; have your eyesight tested regularly – poor eyesight can cause accidents; occasional medical check-ups may be sensible; take precautions against sexually transmitted diseases and AIDS.

6

Financial Matters

Before you move abroad you need to work out the financial implications, and this means taking appropriate advice, particularly if there is a good deal of money at stake. The choice of adviser or advisers is crucial.

It is unwise to assume that your local bank manager, insurance broker or solicitor is in a position to advise you on expatriate financial matters. Expatriate finance is a complex subject, and the chances of finding an expert in this field in your local high street are slim. However, most high street banks and other finance houses have departments, usually based in the Channel Islands, that cater for expatriate customers.

You really need to ask around, look in the advertisement columns of expatriate newspapers and magazines (eg *Resident Abroad*) or ask professional institutes such as the Institute of Chartered Accountants and the British Insurance and Investments Brokers Association to recommend someone. The directory at the end of this book suggests a few contacts.

Good advice does not necessarily come cheap; but on the other hand, not to take good advice could cost you dear. You need to find out how to

- minimise tax liability
- maximise the return from your investments
- provide for emergencies.

A move abroad represents a radical change in your circumstances and your current financial arrangements will probably need a complete rethink.

There are three areas that you need to consider in turn:

- taxation
- investment
- insurance.

The ideal adviser is a person who can deal with all three, particularly where large amounts of money are involved. However, this is not always possible; an accountant may be able to advise you on taxation, but may have to refer you to someone else for advice on investment and insurance.

TAXATION

'In this world nothing can be said to be certain, except death and taxation,' wrote Benjamin Franklin. Anyone planning to retire abroad ought to bear this in mind, particularly the bit about taxation.

There is no reason to pay more tax than you need, and if you do not have to pay any at all, so much the better. People who have resided in Britain for most of their lives generally know the rules of the game – about allowances you can make against tax, tax-free investments and so on.

But if you move aboard your tax circumstances may change. You may find that you no longer need to pay UK tax, but you may be taxed by the authorities in your adopted country. Whatever your situation, you will not want to pay more tax than you really need, hence the need to clarify your position at the outset with Inland Revenue booklet IR20: *Residents and Non-residents. Liability to tax in the UK.*

In the next few pages I attempt to explain some of the ground rules as they exist at present. However, you should bear in mind that at any time the rules may be changed, and that each person's circumstances are different. Moreover, you will have to accept the fact that you are unlikely to escape paying taxes completely.

The importance of being non-resident
Some expatriates believe that once you leave the UK your

obligations to the British tax authorities cease automatically. Wrong.

Even if you have decamped to a remote tropical island, you should not assume that you have escaped the clutches of the Inland Revenue. If the taxman decides that you are resident in the United Kingdom, you remain a UK taxpayer.

As you sit beneath the palm tree sipping pineapple juice ask yourself the following questions:

- Am I going to be in the UK for more than 183 days in one tax year?

- Am I going to spend on average more than 90 days a year in the UK over a period of four years?

- Do I plan to spend any time in the UK and have accommodation available for my use (a place of abode) there?

If the answer to any of these questions is 'yes', add a dollop of gin to your juice and prepare yourself for a shock. In the eyes of the Inland Revenue you are still a UK resident, and therefore a taxpayer. True, the taxman is unlikely to turn up on the doorstep of your beachside villa in person, but he will probably catch up with you in the end.

The third question may need some explaining. If you have a house, flat or just a room available for your use in the UK and you visit the country, you will be regarded as a resident. This remains true even if you do not use the accommodation or only stay in Britain for five minutes.

You may hear of people with property in the UK who have managed not to pay tax to the Inland Revenue. However, their circumstances may be different from yours. For instance, they may have a full-time job abroad, or they may have let their property on a long-term basis.

How to establish non-resident status
You need to demonstrate to the Inland Revenue that you intend to live abroad for a tax year or more. If successful,

you will be offered provisional non-resident status, which means that from the day following departure you will have no liability to UK tax on any income arising outside the UK.

However, if the Inland Revenue have reason to doubt your intention to move abroad on a permanent basis, you may not acquire this status immediately. If, for instance, you still retain a property or continue to engage in business in the UK, it may be difficult to establish the permanency of your expatriation.

In order to avoid liability to capital gains tax you should ensure that chargeable assets are disposed of after your departure from the UK and that you remain a non-resident for a minimum of 36 months. Self-employed people should take advice on when to cease business and when to dispose of their assets. (Incidentally, the sale of your main residence in the UK is not subject to CGT.)

An income tax free existence?

So, you have established your non-resident status. Does this mean that all your income is your own? How marvellous it would be if this were true! In fact, you will still be liable to the Inland Revenue for tax on income arising in the UK with few exceptions.

Pensions, dividends, interest, royalties
Any of these sources of income arising in the UK is normally taxed, although certain British government funds as well as PEPs and ISAs are exempt. In some cases it is possible to have interest paid without tax deducted, but you are still liable for UK tax on it. However, if you are a resident of a country with which the UK has a double taxation agreement you may be able to claim partial relief or exemption.

Since the conditions for exemption or relief vary from agreement to agreement, the best plan is to contact the Inspector of Foreign Dividends who will send you details of the agreement and the relevant claims form. (More on pages 81–82.)

Income from property
Any income from property rentals in the UK is taxable, once it reaches a certain level. Tax must be deducted from the rental income quarterly and paid to the Inland Revenue either by

- the letting agent, or
- the tenant, where there is no letting agent.

It is, of course, possible to offset some of the tax against expenses you have incurred on the property, and by applying to the Financial Intermediaries and Claims Office (FICO) it may be possible for you to receive your rental income with no deduction of tax. Inland Revenue Leaflet IR140 *Non-resident landlords, their agents and tenants* provides information on this matter.

Many expatriates endeavour to reduce their income tax liability by moving their investments offshore. The Channel Islands and the Isle of Man have a large number of financial institutions serving the expatriate, many of them subsidiaries of banks and finance houses on the mainland; and there are others in Luxembourg, the Caribbean, Gibraltar and elsewhere.

It would be sensible to contact a few of these to find out what services they can offer, but, as always, I urge you to seek appropriate advice before you commit yourself.

Inheritance tax and capital gains tax
Do not overlook the matter of UK inheritance tax if your assets exceed the current allowance (around £250,000). You could avoid payment if you declare your new country of residence to be your domicile of choice, but this will take effect only after three years. It may be possible to put any assets in the UK into an offshore company or trust, but you will require advice on this matter.

Capital gains liability should not be overlooked. If you sell a business or a second property you could find yourself faced with a hefty capital gains tax bill from the Inland Revenue, and you should therefore take advice from an accountant as to how to reduce your liability, especially if a large amount is involved.

One idea is to delay the realisation of your capital gains until you are no longer a UK resident. However, unless you are planning to set up house in a tax haven, you may well find the tax authorities in your new country of residence taking an unhealthy interest in your gains.

Taxation abroad

As a general rule the income tax threshold (ie the point at which you start to pay tax on your income) is higher in most other countries than in the UK. As a result, a good many retired British expatriates escape paying income tax in their country of residence.

On the other hand, what other governments lose on the swings they may recoup on the roundabouts and you could find yourself liable for other forms of taxation – even in so-called tax havens. Many European countries, for instance, rely more heavily on indirect taxation, and you would find yourself paying a higher rate of VAT on a wider range of goods than in the UK.

You might also have to pay a wealth tax based on the value of your house or a foreign resident's tax. If you eventually sell it at a profit, you could find yourself paying capital gains tax or even VAT. And don't forget that there are bound to be local taxes as well.

It is impossible in a book of this size to discuss the relative merits of the tax regimes in different countries of the world. For one thing, tax legislation never stands still. To find out the current tax rates before you leave you need to contact either the embassy or consulate of your country of destination or consult an adviser on expatriate finance. The latest edition of Ernst & Young's *Worldwide Personal Tax Guide* is another source of information.

Double taxation agreements

Is there a risk of being taxed twice on the same income or capital? There is, but fortunately Britain has signed double taxation agreements with a number of countries in order to overcome this problem allowing you exemption or partial relief from UK tax on certain types of income and capital gains.

However, you should bear in mind that double taxation agreements may differ from country to country and the precise conditions for exemption or relief vary. You and your advisers therefore need to study the relevant agreement with care. These are available for study at the Inland Revenue Library at Somerset House or from the Inspector of Foreign Dividends.

If you are spending time in two or more different countries the situation becomes more complicated, and the following questions need to be asked to determine which country you will pay taxes to:

- In which country do you have a permanent home?
- Which country is the main centre of your life?
- In which country are you habitually resident?
- Of which country are you a national?

If you are living abroad, you may nonetheless be able to claim certain UK tax allowances. The Inland Revenue Claims Branch (International) will be able to advise you on which – or the Public Departments (Foreign Section) if you receive a pension from Crown service.

What if I remain a UK resident?

Some people will be chary about selling up in the UK, and expect to make the occasional visit to their home. If you decide to share your time between your UK and foreign residence – this might happen if you buy a property in the USA, for example – you will continue to be liable for UK income tax and of course local taxes.

Provided there is a double taxation agreement between the UK and the other country in which you are residing you should be spared two income tax bills, but you will still be liable for local taxes and charges in both countries.

Countries with which the UK has double taxation agreements

European Union countries, Antigua and Barbuda, Argentina, Australia, Azerbaijan, Bangladesh, Barbados, Belarus, Belize, Bolivia, Botswana, Brunei, Bulgaria, Burma (Myanmar), Canada, China, Croatia, Cyprus, Czech Republic, Egypt, Estonia, Falkland Islands, Fiji, Gambia, Ghana, Grenada, Guyana, Hungary, Iceland, India, Indonesia, Israel, Ivory Coast, Jamaica, Japan, Kazakhstan, Kenya, Kiribati, Korea (South), Latvia, Lesotho, Macedonia, Malawi, Malaysia, Malta, Mauritius, Mexico, Mongolia, Montserrat, Morocco, Namibia, New Zealand, Nigeria, Norway, Oman, Pakistan, Papua New Guinea, Philippines, Poland, Romania, Russia, St Kitts and Nevis, Sierra Leone, Singapore, Slovakia, Slovenia, Solomon Islands, South Africa, Sri Lanka, Sudan, Swaziland, Switzerland, Thailand, Trinidad and Tobago, Tunisia, Turkey, Tuvalu, Uganda, Ukraine, USA, Uzbekistan, Venezuela, Vietnam, Yugoslavia, Zambia, Zimbabwe.

INVESTMENTS

When doing research for this book I heard of some unfortunate cases of elderly British people whose financial situation was extremely precarious. The crux of the problem was that their pensions were hardly sufficient to cover their day-to-day living expenses and they had no savings to fall back on.

In the UK there are supplementary benefits which provide a safety net for people whose capital and income fall below a certain level. However, this type of scheme is by no means universal, and so you may need to provide your own safety net. This means ensuring that you have a reasonable amount of capital in addition to your pension(s) and that it is carefully invested. This will help avoid two potentially disastrous scenarios:

- The buying power of your state and company pensions fails to keep up with the cost of living. This could happen as a result of changes in the exchange rate, inflation, because your pension is frozen, or through a combination of these factors.

HOW MUCH ARE YOU WORTH?

To help you and your adviser decide how much you will have available to spend on accommodation and to live on you need to evaluate your financial circumstances.

	You	Your spouse
CAPITAL		
Value of current house	_____	_____
Value of contents	_____	_____
National Savings	_____	_____
Value of any other property	_____	_____
Bank accounts	_____	_____
Building society accounts	_____	_____
Unit trusts, PEPs, ISAs	_____	_____
Government stocks	_____	_____
Other fixed-interest securities	_____	_____
Equities	_____	_____
Other securities	_____	_____
Life assurance policies	_____	_____
Other assets	_____	_____
ANTICIPATED INCOME		
State pension	_____	_____
Occupational pension	_____	_____
Personal pension	_____	_____
Interest from bank or building society	_____	_____
Interest from unit trusts, PEPs, ISAs	_____	_____
Interest from government stocks	_____	_____
Other fixed interest	_____	_____
Interest from equities	_____	_____
Interest from other securities	_____	_____
Interest from life insurance policies	_____	_____
Trust income	_____	_____
Rental income	_____	_____
ANTICIPATED OUTGOINGS:		
One-off		
House purchase	_____	_____
House purchase taxes and fees	_____	_____
Removal charges	_____	_____
Car purchase	_____	_____
Regular		
Local taxes	_____	_____
Income tax	_____	_____
Wealth tax	_____	_____
Home maintenance costs	_____	_____
Management charges (in a condominium)	_____	_____
Insurance (car, house, life, medical)	_____	_____
Electricity	_____	_____
Telephone	_____	_____
Water	_____	_____
Gas	_____	_____
Car maintenance and fuel	_____	_____
Car tax	_____	_____
Other transport costs (eg flights to the UK)	_____	_____
Domestic help	_____	_____
Clothing	_____	_____
Food and drink	_____	_____
Entertainment	_____	_____

- The amount of pension paid is reduced. This happens, for instance, to widows when their husband's occupational pension may be reduced by 50%.

Golden rules for investors

Before going abroad it is essential to review your investments thoroughly to make sure they are appropriate to your new circumstances – retirement and overseas residence. You will need to ensure that your capital is accessible and that you are not paying UK income tax on your investment income unless this is unavoidable.

There are two golden rules for investors:

- Don't put all your eggs in one basket.
- Make sure that your investments are arranged by reputable companies.

There are two broad types of investment:

1. Investments that pay out interest on a regular basis but do not appreciate in value (eg bank deposit accounts, building society accounts).

2. Those that will appreciate in value in the long term and usually pay a dividend (eg stocks and shares, unit trusts, investment trusts). Land and property may also appreciate in value and yield an income in rent.

Ideally you should consider having both types of investment. Money on deposit is readily accessible and if you do not need the income for the time being you can always leave it to accumulate. However, inflation can quickly erode the value of any cash you place on deposit and interest rates can go down.

Some people are reluctant to invest in equities or bonds arguing that their value can go down as well as up – which is, of course, true. On the other hand – if the past is any guide – investments in equities will perform better than deposit accounts in the long run.

In order to reduce risk you should invest in a number of companies, perhaps through a unit trust or an investment trust making use of any tax breaks which are available. In time your capital should increase in value and so should your dividends.

You may wonder whether there is any sense in investing in the country where you have decided to settle. Provided there are suitable opportunities this is certainly an idea worth consideration, particularly since you will need to guard against any financial loss if the pound drops in value against the currency of your country of residence. However, a better idea might be to aim for an investment portfolio with a wide geographical spread to include Europe, North America and the Pacific rim, in order to spend the risk. This can all be arranged from the UK.

Even if you are quite happy with your investment portfolio, it is essential to review it if you are going to be a non-resident for tax purposes. Investments which you made on the strength of tax efficiency may not be quite so suitable when your tax position changes, and any investment adviser you engage needs to bear this in mind. On the other hand, you should not switch round your investments merely for the sake of change.

INDEPENDENT OR TIED ADVICE

In the UK an adviser on life assurance, personal pensions or other financial products may be one of two types:

- An independent financial adviser. He (or she) acts on the client's behalf in recommending a product selected from a range of companies. He may charge for his services and rebate any commission to you. Others, who do not charge, will earn a commission on the product you buy.
- A tied representative of a particular company. He acts on the company's behalf in the sense that he will recommend a product or products selected only from the range offered by that company.

It is important to establish from the outset how independent the advice you are going to receive will be.

If you decide to handle your investments yourself, you should be beware of investment schemes that sound too good to be true (eg funds promising cast-iron security and extremely high returns). My advice is to check the credentials of any financial adviser or firm with whom you plan to do business.

There is no reason why you should not continue to use an investment adviser based in the UK, the Channel Isles or the Isle of Man, where financial services are strictly regulated. Make sure, however, that the firm is approved by the Financial Services Authority.

INSURANCE

Medical insurance

Relatively few countries provide as comprehensive a health service as the UK, and in some cases only those who have subscribed to it all their lives are eligible. It is therefore essential that you investigate the facilities in your prospective country of residence to see if you need to take out private health insurance.

You can choose between

- international medical insurance from a company based in the UK (eg International Private Healthcare Ltd, Exeter Friendly Society, BUPA, Private Patients Plan).

- a medical insurance scheme in your country of residence (which may work out cheaper).

For a more detailed discussion of medical care please see Chapter 5.

Life assurance

The main advantage of a life assurance policy is that it offers your partner or dependents immediate access to a sum of money on your death. A basic whole life plan is relatively cheap and will offer an immediate cash payment to your partner or dependents on your death. Such policies should not be confused with life assurance plans which are primarily investment vehicles.

It may be sensible in the case of a married couple for both partners to take out such an insurance.

House and contents insurance

It is always advisable to insure your home. If you are buying the property with a mortgage, the lender will doubtless insist on this, and in countries like France it is obligatory. In most cases it will be cheaper to insure in your country of residence, but you should nevertheless shop around for the best deal. If you plan to keep on a property in the UK, see if your insurance company in Britain is prepared to insure your property abroad as well at a reduced rate.

You will need to tell your insurer whether you will be residing in your property on a permanent basis or not. Be prepared for higher premiums, an increase in excess figures and exclusion clauses if

- the home is left unfurnished for a certain period
- the home is unoccupied for a certain period (typically more than one or two months at a time)
- the home or part of it is let or sublet.

Typical exclusions are:

- theft
- water damage
- accidental breakage of glass
- malicious damage.

The insurers may also make certain stipulations, for example that water, gas and electricity are turned off at the mains and the water system drained off when the place is unoccupied.

Conditions may be less stringent, however, if arrangements have been made for the property to be visited regularly by a neighbour or agent during your absence, or if it is on a managed estate.

Car insurance

If you are travelling to Europe in your own car you will need to obtain a green card from your insurance company, though this will only cover you for a limited period. You should inform your insurers that you are going to live abroad and find out the insurance position.

Normally they will not insure you unless they have an agent in the country concerned. If they do, you may well find that your insurance premium rises because of the higher risk of accidents and theft in certain countries. You may well find that the terms of the insurance differ from the policies that you are used to in the UK, and you should check the details very carefully.

7

Preparations for Departure

CHECKLIST

Banking; cancellations and disconnections; car; children; electoral registration; financial planning; forwarding of mail; language training; legal advice; your home in the UK; medical matters; National Insurance; passport and visa; pensions; pets; removals; travel arrangements; your will.

If you are leaving Britain for good, you will need to start preparing for the move weeks, perhaps even months, in advance. This chapter lists the most important points, but does not claim to be definitive. Personal circumstances will dictate which matters are of relevance to you.

BANKING

Transfer of funds
If you are buying a property abroad you will need to enlist the aid of your bank or a currency broker at an early stage in the proceedings to transfer cash from one country to another (see Chapter 4). Note that transfers across national boundaries may take longer than you expect.

Bridging loan or mortgage
Many people hope to finance the purchase of their retirement residence from the proceeds of the sale of their house in the UK. Until the latter is sold you may need to borrow from a bank or building society (see Chapter 4). You will need to explore the relative merits and costs of a bridging loan and a short-term mortgage.

Foreign currency and travellers' cheques

It is sensible to obtain foreign currency and travellers' cheques to tide you over the first few days abroad. Credit cards and cash cards are also widely accepted abroad.

Maintaining your account

It makes sense to keep your UK account open, even if you decide to remit the bulk of your cash abroad; there will be times when you may find it more convenient to write a sterling cheque. You need, however, to ensure that the account is kept topped up (eg by having your pension paid into the account) in order to deal with any direct debits you have to fulfil. (Incidentally, this is a good time to review your regular payments.)

Arranging for banking facilities abroad

If you have not yet made arrangements your bank can put you in touch with a bank at your destination abroad or provide a letter of introduction.

Other matters

Most banks offer other services (eg insurance, investment advice) and can act as your executor. However, you may well have other organisations dealing with these matters.

Don't forget to give your bank a contact address.

CANCELLATIONS AND DISCONNECTIONS

You will need to cancel

- milk deliveries
- newspaper deliveries
- subscriptions to magazines or clubs you are no longer interested in
- rentals (eg TV)
- credit agreements.

You will also need to notify the companies providing the following services of your date of departure and arrange for the payment of bills:

- electricity
- gas
- telephone
- water.

CAR

If you are a car driver, you will doubtless wish to have your own private transport in your overseas location. There are various options open to you.

Take your present car out with you

This is a good idea if you are relocating to somewhere in Europe which is a driveable distance from the UK. However, you need to consider the age of the car: if it is several years old, it will cost more to maintain, and obtaining spare parts could be a problem. You will also need to make sure that it complies with regulations in the country where you plan to reside, since modification could prove expensive, and check whether any taxes or import duties will be payable. The embassy or consulate of the country in question should be able to give you the latest information.

The Department of Transport leaflet V526 gives details of how to export a car you already own. If you are taking it out for more than a year, when you actually leave you should complete Section 2 on the back of the Vehicle Registration Document and send it to the Driver Vehicle and Licensing Centre in Swansea. You may be lucky enough to get a refund of excess duty paid.

Buy a new car in the UK

If you have sufficient ready cash there is much to be said for purchasing a new car which is more in line with your needs (eg has right-hand drive for continental motoring, is more economical, is more environmentally friendly). It is possible to buy a car in the UK free of VAT provided you export it within six months; your car dealer can provide you with the necessary VAT Form 410.

You should specify where you intend to use the car and the agent will ensure that you get a model which complies with the legal requirements of the country in question. You also need to ensure that there are local agents for the car and that spare parts are easily obtainable.

Buy a new car in the country where you intend to live
This is an option well worth considering, especially if you are planning to live a long way from the UK (eg in Australia or South Africa). Indeed, you may find this works out cheaper than buying in the UK and paying transport costs.

In the past the UK has been one of the more expensive countries in Europe for car purchase, and you may find that you can buy more cheaply in the country of retirement or in a third country, such as Holland or Belgium. Clearly it pays to shop around paying regard to the different pricing arrangements and tax rates.

CHILDREN

If you still have children of school age you need to consider their schooling. Where important examinations arc looming it is essential to discuss the options with your offspring, their current teachers and perhaps your local education authority (if they are attending state schools), since efforts need to be made to minimise disruption to their education.

Educating your children abroad
If you decide to take your children with you, do not leave anything to chance. In some countries (eg France) the state schools are excellent; in others standards leave much to be desired, and you will want to educate them privately. Since good private schools are often oversubscribed you need to register your child for a place as early as possible.

Word of mouth is the best form of recommendation, and you should ask people resident in your retirement area for guidance as to which schools are most suitable. The local British embassy or consulate will be able to give you information on English medium schools in the area. Failing this, the European Council of International Schools publishes an annual directory of international schools all over the world which can be consulted in most libraries.

If you decide to have a crack at educating your children yourself, Worldwide Education Services (WES) can provide you with training, materials and support for children up to 13 years old. Otherwise you can investigate correspondence tuition from an organisation like Mercer's College which specialises in correspondence courses up to 'A' Level. Bear in mind that learning by correspondence is not an easy option, and most children prefer to learn in the company of others.

Educating your children in the UK

If you decide to have your children educated privately in the UK, the earlier you contact the school you have in mind the better. There are a number of organisations which can offer you advice, such as Gabbitas Educational Consultants and the Independent Schools Information Service (ISIS). You should also consult *The Parents' Guide to Independent Schools* published by the School Fees Insurance Agency (SFIA).

For a retiree some school fees may seem extortionate, but there is no need to panic. As long as your child remains in the UK he is entitled to free education, and many local education authorities can provide boarding facilities for children whose parents are living abroad. You should approach the LEA, preferably through the principal of your child's current school, at the earliest opportunity to explain your case.

The Department for Education & Skills (DFES) publishes a *Directory of Maintained Boarding Schools*. The State Boarding Information Service can also advise you.

ELECTORAL REGISTRATION

If you wish to vote in elections held in the UK while you are abroad, you need to ask the electoral registration officer of your local district or borough council for a change of address form. This entitles you to vote in any parliamentary, European and local election for the duration of the current electoral register. In order to keep your voting rights in future years you need to contact the nearest British embassy or consulate on your arrival and complete the necessary form.

FINANCIAL PLANNING

This is dealt with in depth in Chapter 6. The earlier you start planning the more beneficial it will be for you, so you should seek out a qualified adviser on expatriate finance at the earliest possible opportunity. If you are unaware of any in your area, contact the local Society of Chartered Accountants or the Practitioner Bureau of the Institute of Chartered Accountants in London. A number of firms are listed in Appendix C.

FORWARDING OF MAIL

No matter how hard you try to let everybody know of your change of address there are always some people and organisations who fall through the net. If you cannot find someone to redirect your mail to your new address (your tenant or the new owner of your property) go to the local post office and ask for the relevant form. Your mail will then be redirected automatically for a specified period for a small fee.

YOUR HOME IN THE UK

One of the major decisions you will have had to make is what to do with your residence in the UK, assuming that you are an owner occupier. Many people decide to sell up in order to finance the purchase of a home abroad. Since there are several excellent books on buying and selling houses and flats in the UK, eg *Which way to buy, sell and move house* (Consumers' Association), this matter is not dealt with here.

What if you decide not to sell immediately? Some people

like the idea of keeping on a UK base – at least for the time being – in case their venture abroad does not turn out as they planned. Below are some suggestions.

Leave the accommodation empty
This is fine provided you can afford to maintain two properties and your UK home is in a part of the country that is reasonably secure. However, your insurance company may increase the premium, and if you have a mortgage, your bank or building society might have qualms. In any case, both organisations should be informed.

Ask someone to look after it for you
This is a sensible option provided you have someone in mind – a relation or friend who might live in it, a helpful neighbour, or an organisation that offers houseminding services, such as Animal Aunts or Homesitters Ltd.

Let it
This is a way of paying for the upkeep of the property and perhaps financing a mortgage, too, providing the lender approves. It is always best if you can find a tenant whom you know and trust, but most people have to settle for strangers. You can either advertise for a tenant yourself or appoint a letting agent to do the work for you. You should check what services the agency can provide.

If you live in an area with a large educational institution you could contact the accommodation officer who may be able to take charge of the letting for you in much the same way as an agent.

If you rent your home in the UK, you will have few problems to attend to. Make sure, however, that you give your landlord plenty of notice of your planned departure.

LANGUAGE TRAINING

It is never too soon to start learning the language of the

country where you plan to reside, if it isn't English. In fact you should get in as much practice as possible before you go. There are several ways of tackling it.

Enrol for a course in the UK
Most local authority colleges and adult education centres offer day and evening courses in the most common foreign languages and these are relatively inexpensive. However, normally you need to start at the beginning of the academic year (ie in September) and such courses tend to proceed at a leisurely pace.

If you are dissatisfied with the tuition available you could enquire whether the authority operates more intensive courses. If not see what private language schools can offer or (if you are in London) contact the cultural centre of the country you are bound for. The Spanish, Italian and French cultural institutes all provide excellent courses.

Enrol for a course abroad
A number of organisations arrange fairly intensive courses of two weeks or more either in groups or on an individual basis.

Find a tutor
This can be a sensible move since you then have the chance of learning at your own pace. The Institute of Linguists or Association for Language Learning may be able to recommend someone in your area.

Teach yourself
This is the hardest way to learn a language and often the least effective since you do not get the opportunity to interact with other speakers. A course with audio cassettes (and perhaps video-tapes) will allow you to hear how the language should be spoken. Such courses are available from the BBC, Linguaphone and a number of other publishers. To find out precisely what is available you would be advised to visit a specialist language bookshop, such as Grant & Cutler or LCL.

A number of local authority colleges now offer self-access courses where you have access to courses on tape – and sometimes videos and computerised learning packages as well.

The handbook *How to Master Languages* offers more detailed advice on learning foreign languages and also lists courses and major course providers. The section of language learning in Appendix C also contains some useful addresses.

LEGAL ADVICE

If you have a solicitor in the UK it is essential that you tell him of your plans and your future address. You will probably engage his services anyway to do your conveyancing in the UK (if you are selling your house) and perhaps to keep an eye on legal matters appertaining to your home abroad. This is a timely moment to make or revise your will (see section on wills below).

MEDICAL MATTERS

You need to investigate whether you need to take any precautionary measures before you leave Britain, and it is sensible to visit those who have looked after your health in recent years. You will find plenty of useful advice on going abroad in the Department of Health booklet *Health Advice for Travellers* obtainable free of charge from chemists, doctors, post offices or by phoning 0800 555777.

The following suggestions will ensure that you get off to a good start.

Have appropriate vaccinations
If you are moving to Europe, North America, Australasia or Japan no special vaccinations are required. For other countries vaccinations are often necessary or advisable, and your course of treatment may need to start as much as two months before your departure.

There are vaccinations against polio, typhoid, hepatitis, yellow fever, cholera, rabies, encephalitis and meningococcal meningitis, but it is highly unlikely that you will require jabs against all of these unless you are planning to live in the heart of the jungle.

Health Advice for Travellers should tell you what you need to know, but if you are unsure you should contact Medical Advisory Services for Travellers Abroad (MASTA), London School of Hygiene and Tropical Medicine, Keppel Street, London WC1E 7HT; tel: (020) 7631 4408. MASTA application forms are also obtainable from some chemists.

Your doctor or local health centre may be able to vaccinate you, but you may find it more convenient to use one of the British Airways Travel Clinics in Birmingham, Edinburgh, Glasgow, Leicester, Manchester Newport Pagnell, Nottingham, Purley, Reading, Stratford on Avon and London. These are linked to the MASTA database. Telephone (020) 7233 6661 for further details.

Visit your doctor
It is sensible to visit your GP to tell him of your plans and ideally have a check-up. If you are on medication make sure that you are given a letter to show customs officers on arrival – just in case they suspect you are a drug peddler – and to the doctor who will treat you abroad. In some cases you may require a medical report for insurance purposes or to satisfy the immigration authorities.

If you are taking up permanent residence in another country you will need to surrender your medical card either to the local Family Practitioner Committee or to the passport official as you leave the country. It is advisable to keep a note of the number in case you return to the UK on a long-term basis.

Visit your dentist
This is a good time to have a dental check-up or arrange to have spare dentures made. Dental treatment can be quite expensive abroad and not all insurance schemes cover it.

Visit the optician

It is also a good idea to have your eyes tested, and if you are going to a sunny clime you may want to have one pair of tinted spectacles.

Forms E121 and E111

If you are going to live permanently in a European Union country you need to obtain Form E121 from the DSS. If you are travelling through the European Union you need to obtain Form E111 which is normally included with the *Health Advice for Travellers* booklet.

NATIONAL INSURANCE

If you are not yet in receipt of a state pension you should contact Social Security for advice on National Insurance contributions. It may be to your advantage to pay voluntary contributions at the Class 3 (non-employed) rate to maintain your UK insurance record for the retirement pension and widow's benefits. These voluntary payments, however, will not necessarily entitle you to social security benefits in your new country of residence, and you will need either to contribute to the state insurance scheme there or to take out private insurance.

Britain has a social security agreement with a number of different countries but the terms of the agreements vary. Make sure you obtain a copy of the relevant leaflet from the Benefits Agency Overseas Branch in Newcastle upon Tyne.

PASSPORT AND VISA

Make certain your passport is valid. If you need to obtain a passport or renew it, ask for a form at your local post office and send it off to the appropriate passport office. Expect a wait of up to a month, at least. If you need it more urgently you will have to visit the office yourself.

Passport agency office addresses are listed in Appendix C.

For many countries a passport alone will normally suffice for a visit of up to three months, but if you are planning to take up permanent residence abroad in a country outside the European Economic Area you will probably need to obtain a special visa before you leave.

You should contact the relevant embassy or consulate some time before your departure and preferably before you make a purchase to discover whether you will be eligible for residence status. You may find that you are not – in the case of the USA or Australia, for instance – unless you are able to comply with certain requirements.

If all is well, you will need to find out the correct procedures for obtaining the right type of visa. You can, if you wish, employ a third party to make the arrangements for you, but you may be required to attend the embassy or consulate in person at some stage.

Together with your passport you will have to produce some or all of the following items:

- a birth certificate

- a marriage certificate if applicable

- evidence of financial status

- a medical report

- photographs.

PENSIONS AND OTHER BENEFITS

Inform your local social security office of your plans and anticipated address at the earliest possible opportunity and specify how you are to be paid. The administrators of any private or occupational pension fund you are a member of should also be informed of your movements. (This matter is dealt with more fully in Chapter 5.)

PETS

If you decide to take your pet or pets with you, you must first check the rules and regulations of the country you are going to. While taking pets from the UK into Europe has become somewhat easier with the introduction of PETS certificates (the so-called pet passports), a number of countries further afield require you to obtain an import permit and may impose a period of quarantine.

You will need some or all of the following documentation:

- an official PETS certificate (known as the pet passport);

- an official export health certificate signed by a local veterinary inspector (this is mandatory for pets entering certain European countries and all long-haul countries participating in the PETS scheme; a different type of certificate is necessary for pets going to France);

- a private veterinary health certificate (for the Netherlands);

- a rabies vaccination certificate (for Benelux, Germany and Switzerland);

- an import permit (for a number of countries including Australia, Cyprus, Malta, New Zealand and several Caribbean countries, obtainable from your destination country).

For further information you should contact the PETS Helpline: 0870 241 1710 or www.defra.gov.uk/animalh.

There are a number of organisations which specialise in transporting pets abroad, and some addresses will be found in the directory at the end of this book. The RSPCA publishes a leaflet on taking pets abroad.

If you decide not to take them with you, and are unable to find a good home for them, there are several animal charities that may be able to take them off your hands (eg Cats Protection Society, National Canine Defence League).

Your local telephone directory will list your nearest branch. Alternatively, if you are only planning to be away for a matter of months you could find someone to look after your pets (and perhaps your house, too) in your absence. Animal Aunts is one organisation that offers such a service.

REMOVALS

If you are leaving Britain for good there will be considerable soul-searching in the matter of personal effects. You have to decide what to take with you and what to dispose of. Remember that the more you decide to take the greater the cost of the move. As for shipping all your household furniture to Australia or the Caribbean, the cost is likely to be prohibitive.

When deciding what to take you should ask yourself the following questions:

- How much can be accommodated in the new residence? If you are moving from a four-bedroomed house to a two-bedroomed apartment, you will need to jettison at least half your personal effects.

- What would it cost to re-equip on arrival? You need to compare the cost of moving all your possessions abroad with the cost of furnishing your residence from local sources, if this is indeed possible. In some cases you will need to re-equip: there is little point in moving your kitchen stove and your refrigerator if they are on their last legs. In any case, some of your equipment may be incompatible (eg UK television sets and video-recorders in France, all electrical equipment in the USA).

- What will it cost to move all your personal effects? Moving a full load of furniture from the UK to Southern Europe is unlikely to be less than £3,000 and could amount to £4,000 or more. However, many removal firms offer the option of part loads for smaller quantities, where the truck carries the personal effects of a number of clients moving to the same area. Bear in mind that if you are moving to a member state of the European Union VAT is payable.

Moving one's personal effects from one country to another is not just a matter of loading them onto a truck and taking them off at the other end. You will probably find it easiest to entrust the task to an international removal firm, preferably one that is bonded by the British Association of Removers (Overseas Group), the Federation of International Furniture Removers (FIDI) or the Overseas Moving Network Inc (OMNI). Most will offer a comprehensive service which entails:

- advice on and assistance with your documentation (including translations where necessary);
- packing (bear in mind that the insurance policy will not usually cover breakable items if they are owner packed);
- collection and loading into van;
- transport door to door;
- customs clearance (this formality is no longer required for most EU countries);
- delivery, unpacking and setting up;
- removal of unwanted materials;
- storage, if required;
- comprehensive insurance cover;
- preparation of an inventory.

TRAVEL ARRANGEMENTS

If you have your own transport and are settling in Europe you may well find it most convenient to travel by car. You can then take some of your smaller personal effects with you for use on arrival. At holiday times it is sensible to book your ferry or Channel Tunnel crossing in advance.

If you suffer from a physical handicap, the *Holidays and Travel Abroad Guide* produced by the Royal Association for Disability and Rehabilitation (RADAR) will prove very useful. For long distances you will probably find it most convenient to travel by air.

YOUR WILL

In order to facilitate the disposal of your assets on your death it is important to make a will which reflects your new circumstances – and this applies to your partner as well.

Your solicitor will need to take into account the law of the country in which you will be residing in order to reduce the amount of inheritance tax or death duties for which you might be liable. Another consideration is that some countries impose restrictions on the disposal of your property (as is the case in Scotland) and a proportion of your estate has to be left to your spouse or children.

It may well be necessary for you to make two wills – one to apply to your assets in the UK and the other to those in the country of residence – in order to facilitate the administration of your estate and also to cut down on costs. There can be a considerable delay in disposing of your assets if your UK will has to be authenticated to the satisfaction of the foreign authorities.

Making a second will will often work out less expensive in the long run than having a complicated English will recognised by the authorities abroad with all the costs involved. Moreover, if matters regarding your estate are not settled within six months of your death in Spain or Italy, for instance, a tax surcharge may be payable.

A number of the firms listed in the legal services section of Appendix C have expertise in drafting both English and foreign wills.

CHECKLIST

This should help to remind you of the matters you need to see to. Not all will be applicable to your circumstances.

Arrange letting or sale of house
Bank
Benefits Agency
Car
Circulate new address
Credit or charge card company
Dentist
Disposal of surplus personal effects
District council: pay council tax and any other dues
Doctor: check-up; prescription
Electricity: give at least 48 hours' notice
Financial advice
Gas: give at least 48 hours' notice
Insurance
Landlord (if a tenant): give notice according to terms of
    contract
Library: return books
Magazine subscriptions: cancel or have redirected
Medical card: surrender to immigration official
Milkman: cancel
Newspaper deliveries: cancel
Optician
Pension administrator
Passport
Post Office: forwarding of mail
Rental or HP agreements: terminate
Savings: notify organisations of change of address (eg
    National Savings Office, Premium Bond Office,
    stockbroker, etc)
Solicitor
Storage of personal effects
Visa
Telephone: give at least 7 days' notice.
Transport of personal effects
Travel arrangements
Water company
Will

8

Settling In

You may imagine that once you arrive in your new home you can sit back and enjoy yourself. Not a bit of it! In the first few weeks you will have to get organised, and this can mean time spent at local council offices or with the police dealing with residence permits, tax and so on. Let's look at those matters which will need to occupy your attention during the first few weeks.

BANKING

If you are taking up permanent residence you are almost certainly going to need to open a bank account. You may already have used a bank in the foreign country for the transfer of funds to pay for your new home, and you can, of course, open an account there provided it is convenient.

However, first of all it is sensible to ask other expatriates which banks they use: it clearly makes sense to use a bank which is used to handling the accounts of foreigners. Although many banks throughout the world offer cheque books, standing orders, cash cards and credit cards, not all of them do so and the service can vary considerably from one bank to another.

In order to open a bank account you may have to provide proof of residence and a declaration of your income. A reference from your bank in the UK can sometimes come in handy. Note that banking law differs from country to country, and in some places you are actually breaking the law if you run up an overdraft, and your account could be frozen.

BRITISH CONSULATE/EMBASSY

Sooner or later (and preferably sooner) it makes good sense to register with the local British consulate. If you have problems with the authorities the consul may be able to intervene, and he is a person you may need to contact in an emergency. If you are involved in an accident or civil disorder, or become entangled with the law, the consul should be called in. He can also register births, marriages and deaths.

Consulates can provide you with useful information (eg English-speaking doctors, lawyers, hospitals, churches), put you in touch with expatriate self-help organisations in the vicinity, and advise you on your voting rights in the UK.

Under the Representation of the People Act 1989 you may register as an overseas voter in the constituency where you usually vote, and for this you need to obtain an overseas elector's form from the consulate. This must be completed, witnessed and returned before 10 October if you wish to be included on the electoral register which comes into effect on 16 February of the following year. You will be eligible to vote in all parliamentary and European elections, but not in local elections in the UK.

CAR

If you have imported a car into the country you will normally need to register it and get local number plates. In most countries you will need to pay a car tax.

You should also check insurance arrangements. In some countries you have to insure your car with a local insurer – at least for basic third-party insurance. If you can continue to be insured by your UK insurer, you will need to inform him of your change of residence and change of registration number. Do not be surprised to receive an increase in premium, since accident rates are often higher elsewhere.

Note that the rules of the road may differ on the Continent and in North America. In Australia they differ from state to state! Also an increasing number of countries impose on-the-spot fines for traffic offences. Drivers are often required to carry a warning triangle, a spare set of lights and a first-aid kit in the car and you should always keep your driving licence and insurance certificate with you.

CHURCH

Even if you do not regard yourself as particularly devout, there is much to be gained from making contact with the local expatriate church, synagogue or mosque, especially if you are living outside the English-speaking world. This is an ideal place to meet fellow expatriates and, if necessary, seek help.

The Anglican church has chaplaincies all over the world whose prime purpose is to minister to English-speaking communities. It is particularly well represented in Europe and welcomes English-speaking Christians of all denominations. In larger centres there may be other churches serving the expatriate community, including Scottish Presbyterian, Baptist and Methodist.

For further information on the church overseas you should contact organisations such as the Church of England Board for Social Responsibility (Overseas Resettlement Secretary), the Church of Scotland Overseas Council or the Methodist Church Overseas Division. The Intercontinental Church Society publishes a useful *Directory of English-Speaking Churches Abroad*.

DRIVING

In many countries you can drive for six months or more on your British driving licence. Eventually you will need to exchange it – perhaps with an accompanying translation – for a local driving licence. This is normally a straightforward procedure: you simply have to show your current British licence and provide a few photographs and perhaps a medical certificate. If you delay, you may be obliged to take a driving test.

LEGAL MATTERS

I have already mentioned the importance of making a will to cover your assets in your new country of residence, since your UK will may not be recognised there or administrative delays may occur in obtaining probate. If you fail to make a will in France, for instance, your beneficiaries may have to pay 60% of the value of the property to the tax authorities.

In some countries the will has to be prepared by a notary and deposited in a central registry, and you may need to appoint a qualified executor rather than a member of your family. Make sure that your executors (and legal advisers) in Britain are kept informed of any foreign wills you make.

If all your assets are in your country of residence you may decide to dispense with your British will. However, you must bear in mind that inheritance laws vary from country to country, and you are not always free to dispose of your assets as you wish. For example, you may have to leave a proportion of your assets to different members of your family.

LOCAL AUTHORITIES

If you are a householder you will doubtless have to register with the local town hall. In parts of Europe this may entail completing forms, providing proof of identity and proof of ownership of the property. Do not be surprised if you are asked for a few photographs as well. In due course, you will receive a demand for payment of local taxes.

RESIDENCE PERMIT

Although you will have been issued in the UK with a residence visa, this is probably valid for only a short time (typically three months from the issue date) so you cannot begin too soon to register with the appropriate authorities, often the local police department. In Italy, you need to register with the police within three days of your arrival.

You will normally have to take your passport with you and supporting documentation. In Spain, for example, you will need to provide

- four passport photographs;
- a certificate from the British consulate that you are resident in Spain;
- a *papel de estado*;
- a certificate from your Spanish bank stating your current bank balance or income;
- evidence that you belong to a private health insurance scheme valid in Spain or are eligible for Spanish national health insurance;
- evidence of accommodation (eg title deeds, rental agreement);
- the first names of your parents.

You may well find that your residence certificate has a finite life and that you have to renew it after a period of years.

SOCIAL SECURITY

If you are receiving a state pension, you may be entitled to state health benefits in your country of residence (and you certainly will be within a member state of the European Union. You will normally have to go to the local branch of the health service and present Form E121 and perhaps other personal documentation (eg birth certificate, passport, marriage certificate). You will then receive a certificate of entitlement and possibly be allocated a doctor.

If you are not yet a pensioner and you wish to make use of the state health system you will need to make regular contributions. In several countries you will not be eligible for state benefits and will have to rely on private insurance.

TAXATION

You should take advice on whether you need to register with the tax authorities and obtain a tax code. If your income falls below a certain threshold you may consider this unnecessary, but bear in mind that some countries impose other taxes (eg a wealth tax, based on the value of your assets) for which you may be liable.

Filling in a tax form can be a problem if it is in a language you do not understand very well, and there may be penalties if it is not submitted in good time. For this reason a number of expatriates engage an accountant to complete the form for them.

UTILITIES

If you have bought a new property from a developer the chances are that arrangements will have been made to connect you up to the electricity, gas and water supply. If not, you will need to contact the different companies involved and arrange for connection, for which a charge may be made. You will normally be required to sign a contract and possibly pay a deposit.

In some countries it is customary to complete a direct debit form which enables the different utilities companies to debit your account when payments become due. This avoids the possibility of disconnection if for some reason your payment is delayed.

YOUR NEW ADDRESS

If you have not already done so you need to notify various people and organisations of your new address. Here are some suggestions:

- next of kin in the UK
- other relations
- friends
- bank or building society in the UK
- solicitor in the UK
- Benefits Agency
- Inland Revenue

- insurance company or broker
- journals to which you subscribe
- pension fund administrator
- tenants or letting agent
- financial adviser.

If you move you will need to go through the same procedure and also include the equivalents in your country of residence.

ACCLIMATISATION

Living in a foreign country is not quite the same as spending a holiday there. Holidays are usually short affairs during which there is no time to get bored because you are surrounded by novelty. But when you are in the same place for years, the novelty wears off, and you need to adjust to your new circumstances.

'Settling in involves trying to understand what is going on and assimilating new ways of doing things before the next stage of settling down arrives. Some people feel challenged to insist on doing things the British way and fail. The key is to accept a different way of life. It is not always easy.'[1]

J A S Abecasis-Phillips' words actually appear in a guide to living in Germany, but the idea they express can be applied to British expatriates in most countries, especially countries that fall outside the Anglo-Saxon tradition – which means most of Europe, for a start.

In non-English speaking countries there is often a communication problem, particularly if your knowledge of the local language is only rudimentary, and it is unwise to assume that everybody will understand you perfectly. If you are prone to making jokes, you should exercise restraint since words spoken in jest might be taken literally by the locals if their standards of humour differ from yours.

Some people try to erect a cordon around themselves in an attempt to create a Little England in the sun. There are, of course, British colonies in Florida whose members hardly ever encounter a real live American despite the absence of any language barrier. This state of affairs may well stem from the fact that people have not really got to grips with their new environment – which, naturally, includes people, as well as climate and scenery.

People in other countries are different, even if their appearance is similar to ours. Their value systems have been shaped by their education, the history of their country, their religion, the attitudes of their leaders (perhaps) and their traditions. This should come as no surprise. We ourselves are a product of a similar process.

Unfamiliar attitudes
The following illustrations demonstrate a few attitudes that may differ from our own:

Attitudes towards authority
In some countries the state appears to have draconian powers, but people are not in the habit of questioning rules and regulations that have been laid down, no matter how illogical they may seem. There may be an underlying fear that if you remove strong controls chaos will ensue.

Attitudes towards time
In some countries punctuality is regarded as a virtue; in others it is a vice. The warmer the climate the less people seem inclined to rush around to meet deadlines. As a retiree you should be happy to adopt a more relaxed attitude towards time.

Attitudes towards privacy
Most British people like to keep their lives private; in other countries participation is the order of the day. People like to do things together rather than alone. This can have advantages, in that complete strangers may be prepared to strike up a conversation with you in trains or restaurants.

Attitudes towards noise
In some countries noise is the inevitable accompaniment to having a good time, and if you complain to the authorities you will be greeted with a blank stare. Perhaps the best

policy to adopt is: 'If you can't beat them, join them.'

Attitudes towards animals
The Koreans eat dogs; we look on them as friends. The French and Italians shoot birds; many English people prefer to watch them. In parts of the world people look on donkeys as just a means of transport, while we might regard them as creatures with feelings. On the other hand, in countries with a poor animal welfare record chickens run about freely while in Britain most are confined to battery cages.

Attitudes towards women
Although women are supposedly emancipated, in some places old habits die hard. The further south you go the more you will find that men are still very dominant. On the other hand, in many such societies age is revered, and a woman retiree may well be treated with considerable courtesy.

Attitudes towards children
The idea that children should be seen and not heard is quite foreign to certain societies abroad. Children are creatures to be cosseted and spoiled, and parents positively dote on their offspring. The idea of leaving them at home when you go out to dine would be anathema to many a Mediterranean parent.

Once you start to recognise such points of difference you are well on your way to understanding the people of the country you have retired to. Their behaviour may sometimes strike you as strange, but just consider how odd British practices may seem to them.

Rather than criticise or kick up a fuss you have to try to meet people on their own terms. Then, instead of remaining an outsider, you will come to be accepted as part of the local community. In other words you will start to feel at home.

REFERENCE

1. *Long stays in Germany*, J A S Abecasis-Phillips (David & Charles).

9

Enjoying a Foreign Lifestyle

DISCOVERING YOUR NEW LIFESTYLE

Retirement calls for a change of outlook, and for some people the transition from a regular work routine to a less structured way of life is not easy. For this reason an increasing number of firms are providing pre-retirement counselling sessions for their staff to enable them to manage the transition effectively. If your life centred on your work you may feel somewhat bereft when the time comes to hang up your boots.

The transition is less abrupt if you have developed interests outside your workplace – as the organiser of a social club, as the leader of a guide troop, as a JP or a local councillor. Many retired people I come across in the UK insist they are more active now than at any time in their lives. However, if you head abroad you turn your back on all this, and will have to build your life completely from scratch.

Forget about the idea of lazing in the sun all day. This may be fine on holiday when you need to unwind from the pressures of everyday life, but people who are used to leading active lives can easily become bored with this kind of existence. The idea of a perpetual holiday with sun, sand and sangria may sound marvellous, but, as I have already mentioned, the novelty can wear off after a time.

Expatriates come in all shapes and sizes. There are loners who prefer to keep themselves to themselves; there are those who wish to live rather as they did in the UK and confine themselves to the expatriate community; there are those who decide to 'go native' and distance themselves from all things British. It would be wrong of me to prescribe how you should spend your retirement, but this chapter offers suggestions.

GET TO KNOW THE COUNTRY

When I worked abroad I was surprised to come across expatriates who knew little, if anything, about the country where they were employed. Admittedly there were some among them who were preoccupied with their work, but there were others who had little interest in their surroundings and regarded their stay abroad as a form of exile. They were just waiting for the day their posting would come to an end.

As a retiree you will have plenty of time to get acquainted with your new surroundings. Fortune always favours the bold, and there are three initial steps you need to take to achieve this goal:

- *Travel.* If you do not have your own transport there are bound to be coach tours, or you can plan your own itinerary by bus or rail with the help of a guide book – such as *Fodor*, *The Blue Guide*, *Baedeker*, *Insight* or *Lonely Planet*. Some national tourist offices and local information bureaux issue travel literature free of charge.

- *Read.* Search out books on the history and traditions of the country and try literary works by local authors. If local bookshops seem to have very little to offer in English, try contacting a bookshop in the UK to see if they offer a mailing service. The Good Book Guide is one organisation which is geared up to sending books abroad. Also investigate local English libraries.

- *Watch.* Watch films that have been made in the country and tune into the local TV station to see what keeps the locals amused. If the programmes are dreadful regard this as part of your education. Go to the theatre, if there is one in the locality, and attend festivals and other events.

LEARN THE LANGUAGE

In order to be able to participate fully in the life of your adopted country, you need to speak the language of its citizens. This will not prove too onerous if you have moved to Australia or Canada, but elsewhere you will need to make an effort.

While you may not become perfect in the language, a working knowledge can be very useful, when you are shopping, dining out, dealing with tradesmen or touring. It will prove indispensable in emergencies – if you are hospitalised or involved in an accident.

Above all, knowledge of the language will do wonders for your social life. The barriers will come down and you are more likely to find yourself accepted, simply because it demonstrates your commitment to the country is long term and you are prepared to blend in with the people.

Ideally you should have already made a start on the language, as recommended in Chapter 7. Whatever the general consensus, it is never too late to start learning a language, and in the UK I have met foreign refugees in their sixties and seventies who have made passable attempts to get to grips with our language, so it is not an impossible task. If you are unsure how to set about learning, you might ask members of the local expatriate community for suggestions.

Most towns – in Europe, at least – have language schools, some of which will have special language classes for foreigners. Local newspapers, particularly English language newspapers, will carry details of these. Alternatively you could look round for a private tutor – ideally someone who has experience of teaching languages to adults.

GET TO KNOW THE LOCAL PEOPLE

One difficulty older people face when they move to a new locality is developing social contacts, simply because they have lost the technique of striking up new friendships. You may feel the problem is compounded if there is a language barrier.

However, the solution lies in your hands. Instead of sitting at home in your 'castle', you need to go out to restaurants and cafés, which perform the role of meeting places in the same way as neighbourhood pubs do in the UK. There may be clubs that you can join, including senior citizen's clubs, sports clubs and Rotary clubs.

Local newspapers and information centres are a useful source of information. In many countries there are expatriate organisations which publish directories of clubs and associations at which you would be welcome.

DEVELOP NEW INTERESTS

Retirement should not be seen as the end of one's existence, but rather the beginning of a new stage in one's life, where you have considerable freedom to do as you wish. You may have had a wide range of interests back home, not all of which you will be able to continue with.

You may develop an interest in the archaeology, the architecture or the wild life of the area where you now live. You may decide to take up new sporting activities – croquet, golf or bowls. Or perhaps the time has come to put your pen to paper and write a novel... or your memoirs.

Where there is a substantial expatriate community you may be called on to sing with the local choral society, act with the amateur dramatic group or help out on the local church committee. You normally find that the people who contribute the most are the ones who derive the greatest satisfaction from life.

In the UK I know many retired people who keep their minds alert by embarking on a course of study, but if you are living abroad you may not always find suitable courses on your doorstep. Should this be a problem, you could investigate distance learning possibilities. The Open University, for instance, has a substantial number of students living abroad.

KEEP IN TOUCH WITH HOME

Few expatriates want to cut themselves off from their roots
entirely when they move abroad. There is always the
possibility that one day you will wish to return, and if you
do not keep up with events the place may be unrecognisable
when the time comes.

You will want to keep in touch with members of your
family and your circle of friends back home, and it is here
that letter writing comes into its own. Sending a letter costs
very little; keeping in touch by phone can work out expensive
and as the bills start to roll in you may find it prudent to
restrict your international calls to a minimum. If you dislike
putting pen to paper, you could communicate by e-mail.

One of the best ways of keeping in touch with events in
Britain and throughout the world is to listen in to the BBC
World Service. In most locations you will need a radio
receiver that picks up short-wave broadcasts – but this does
not have to be expensive. Some years ago I purchased a
small transistor radio with a shortwave band for £20 in the
duty free shop at Heathrow Airport which served me very
well abroad – and continues to serve me well in the UK.

The BBC publishes a monthly programme bulletin called
On Air which is available from British embassies, consulates
and British Council offices or by subscription from the BBC
itself. The Engineering Department at Broadcasting House
can advise if you have trouble in finding the right shortwave
frequency. If you have access to the Internet you will be able
to hear programmes broadcast in the UK.

Satellite transmissions have revolutionised television
broadcasting, and with the appropriate aerial or dish it is
possible to pick up English language transmissions in many
parts of the world. The BBC World Service transmits
television programmes by satellite to certain areas, notably
Asia, and in much of Europe BSkyB, CNN and other
English-language channels are available.

Daily and Sunday newspapers from the UK are on sale in
many of the larger European cities and resorts, though at
higher prices than in Britain itself, and they may well be on

sale a day late. However, if you live in a more remote area there is no need to miss out on the news. You could, for example take out a subscription to a weekly journal such as *The Guardian Weekly, The Weekly Telegraph* or *The Economist.* There are other monthly and bi-monthly journals aimed at the expatriate market, such as *Resident Abroad* and *Expatriate Today.*

If you want to keep in touch with the locality you come from do not overlook regional and county magazines as well as local weekly newspapers which usually operate a mailing service. But bear in mind that a number of local papers – as well as the national dailies – have their own websites that publish the main news stories of the day. You can log on to these via the Internet from virtually any part of the world. Addresses can be found in Benn's *Media Directory, Whitaker's Almanack* or the *Writer's & Artist's Yearbook* (A & C Black). Some people abroad subscribe to the local church magazine of the locality where they used to live.

EAT SENSIBLY

We are what we eat, according to one school of thought, so if we want to enjoy good health we need to eat healthy food. On the other hand, nobody wants to pay through the nose for the privilege.

It is therefore sensible to take stock of your diet when you take up residence in a new country, as modifications may be in order. In a warmer clime you may find lighter meals more to your taste, and you may not find all your favourite foods readily available in the local shops. Where they are obtainable they may appear dreadfully expensive.

Rather than import your British eating habits lock, stock and barrel, why not investigate what the locals eat? Around the Mediterranean incidents of heart disease are much lower than in the UK, and the reason often given is that southern Europeans have a healthier diet.

Dieticians recommend that you eat

- MORE fruit, vegetables, beans, potatoes, pasta, rice, cereals, bread, fish, herbs, spices;

- LESS fatty meat, dairy produce, salty food, fried food (though olive oil is relatively healthy because it is unsaturated).

If you suffer from diabetes, allergies or other complaints you will need to follow your doctor's advice on what types of food you should avoid.

In hot climates particular attention needs to be paid to food hygiene.

Salads are very healthy for you, but the ingredients must be washed thoroughly. Extra care needs to be taken with food storage: fresh food needs to be stored at the proper temperature and if you are plagued with power cuts it makes sense to buy food on a daily basis rather than risk infection.

Finally, a note about drinking. Wine in moderation with a meal is excellent for most people since it aids digestion, an occasional brandy or Scotch does you no harm either, and what better on a stifling day than a glass of cold beer. However, don't overdo it. However pleasant it may seem to live in an alcoholic haze, it wreaks havoc on your constitution.

One needs to take care with tapwater. In much of Europe, Australasia and North America it is quite safe to drink – as safe as the bottled water you get in restaurants and supermarkets. Elsewhere you may not be quite so lucky. If you have any doubts about the water, boil it.

KEEP FIT AND HEALTHY

If the climate is good you will need little persuading to go out and take exercise, even if it is of the gentlest type. But take care not to overdo things: three-hour long tennis matches at the age of 75 could cause you some injury or strain.

One needs to take of one's health. Wounds and grazes need to be dressed quickly before they become infected; prolonged exposure to the sun should be avoided, and you should use protective creams; if you have an accident or suddenly fall ill, make sure you get medical attention with all due speed.

You will find further tips on keeping healthy in Chapter 5.

FINDING WORK

If you are moving abroad in order to work, the companion volume to this book, *Getting a Job Abroad* will prove more relevant to your purpose. However, there are people who after retirement are suddenly presented with a job opportunity which they feel they cannot turn down.

Paid employment

If you are offered a job on a part-time, casual or full-time basis you need to check with the authorities that you are allowed to take it up under the terms of your residence permit.

In the USA, for instance, taking paid employment if you do not possess the appropriate work visa can lead to deportation. It may be possible to have your visa changed to enable you to work, but you must proceed through the correct channels and this can take time.

If you have a job offer before you leave Britain it is essential to show your letter of appointment to the embassy or consulate issuing the visa. (See also Chapter 12.)

Self employment

Again, you need to investigate the terms of your residence visa. Even if you are planning to set up as an odd job person you may have to obtain a licence to do so and register with the tax authorities. The precise requirements differ from country to country and you should certainly take legal advice if you are considering forming a company or partnership.

There are some places where self-employment may bring unforeseen benefits. In the USA, for instance, you may be able to get a temporary visa which will enable you to live in the country the whole year round.

Voluntary work

No restrictions are usually put on voluntary (ie unpaid) work, but you should check up on this. If by doing a job for no reward you deprive someone else of a paid job, the authorities may decide to step in.

10

Dealing with Emergencies

Living abroad can be immensely pleasurable as long as
everything runs smoothly. But what if things start to go
wrong? What if your partner dies, what if the money runs
out, what if a storm or a hurricane wrecks your house, what
if you fall seriously ill and there is no one to look after
you...?

Problems like this can occur in Britain, of course, but at
home you are equipped to deal with them. In a foreign land
they can be more unnerving, especially if you have no close
relations in the vicinity, you are unfamiliar with procedures
in the country and do not speak the language.

Many of us like to assume that disasters always strike
other people, never ourselves. However, it is wise to be
prepared. You need to have close by you – or on your
person when you are out and about – the following items:

- a list of telephone numbers that you can contact in an
  emergency – this would include your bank, the British
  consulate, chaplain or priest, close relations, credit card
  agency, doctor, electrician, emergency services, insurance
  broker or company, next of kin, plumber, solicitor;

- passport or identity card – with your current address on,
  your social security number, your driving licence;

- details of any medication you are taking, allergies (eg to
  penicillin), any serious medical condition;

- a phrase book (if you are in a non-English speaking
  country and you do not speak the local language well).

In a number of countries expatriate self-help organisations
produce information booklets that suggest how you should

cope with almost every eventuality, and are usually based on experience gleaned over a period of years.

ACCIDENTS

These happen to the best of us whether we are in the house, out on the road, up a mountain or playing a quiet game of golf. Even if the injury does not appear serious, you should not rely just on emergency first-aid treatment, but make an appointment to see a doctor or specialist. If you are bitten or scratched by an animal in a country where rabies is endemic (eg continental Europe) you ought to have an anti-rabies vaccination.

Road accidents are particularly traumatic and if it is a particularly serious or fatal accident, you may need to contact the nearest British consul. As in the UK you must try to keep your cool and should not admit liability. Contact your insurance company as quickly as possible to find out what you should do if your car is damaged. Don't overlook your health: you may be suffering from shock and need hospital treatment.

CULTURE SHOCK

This is a very unpleasant phenomenon which you may experience quite soon after your arrival. You get frustrated with delays, you have visions of being robbed, and suffer from an extreme form of homesickness. You feel depressed or overstressed; you get headaches and feel confused, isolated and powerless; you start to find fault with everything and everyone.

Adapting to a new environment, alas, takes its toll, and the initial period in a new country can be particularly stressful. Rather than resort to sedatives or the bottle you need to recognise that this is merely a passing phase, and as you start to feel your way around and begin to understand your new environment better, you will start to feel at home.

Culture shock normally goes through five phases:

- *the honeymoon stage* – this is the stage most tourists experience. You are intrigued and enthusiastic about everything you see and the people you meet;

- *crisis and disintegration* – you feel lost, isolated, lonely and inadequate and tend to become very withdrawn;

- *reintegration* – you become more self-assertive and start to find fault with the country and its people;

- *autonomy* – you begin to find that you can cope with the new situations and become more relaxed and sympathetic;

- *independence* – at last you feel at home accepting and relishing the cultural and social differences.

Not every expatriate experiences culture shock, and the way to avoid it is to come well prepared. The better you understand the culture and values (and language) of the local people the better you will cope with your new circumstances.

DEATH

The death of a partner can be traumatic wherever it occurs, and you will need all the support you can get. With luck some member of your family will take charge of the arrangements, but if not the local community will doubtless rally round with help and advice.

Even if you are not a member of any church, it is a good idea to contact the nearest chaplain or English priest. He will be able to assist with funeral arrangements and offer advice on where the deceased can be laid to rest.

If your partner has chosen to end their days on foreign soil, you may well feel it is entirely appropriate for him or her to be buried there too. A second important consideration is that sending the body back to the UK for burial is expensive and sometimes impracticable.

Most countries now have crematoria so if you desire a

funeral or memorial service in the UK, it may well be possible to have the body cremated locally and the ashes sent home. Sending the body to Britain for cremation is an expensive option, especially if the deceased has to be transferred into a British type of coffin on arrival at the undertaker's in the UK. Spanish coffins, for instance, are not accepted in British crematoria.

Deciding your own future can prove tricky. If you have no relatives in the vicinity, some of them may well suggest that you return to the UK where someone will be able to keep an eye on you. However, if your health is good, you enjoy life abroad, your financial situation is sound and you have a circle of friends you can turn to, there is no reason why you should not stay put – at least for a time.

People you need to inform

- British consulate (who will notify the General Register Office in the UK and issue a death certificate).
- The deceased's lawyer.
- The administrators of the deceased's pension fund.
- The social security office (who will need to make adjustments to the pension).
- Your next of kin.
- Appropriate local authorities.
- An undertaker.
- The deceased's insurance company (who will pay out on a life assurance policy).
- The deceased's bank.
- The deceased's financial adviser.

DISABILITY

In some countries it is assumed that looking after the disabled is the responsibility of the person's family, especially in southern Europe, and the concept of sheltered housing is slow in catching on. People who become disabled and live alone usually have to employ a nurse and domestic staff out of their own funds.

Residential homes exist abroad, but most of them have catered for the nationals of the country. However, where there is a large concentration of retired expatriates, eg the Spanish costas, change is in the air, and there are now a few sheltered housing developments and rest homes built with retired expatriates in mind.

For some very elderly, handicapped people the best option is to return to the UK to be with their families or to go into a nursing home. If the thought of returning to the British climate appals you, you could investigate if any nursing facilities are available locally. In many cases you will have to pay for nursing home accommodation out of your own resources.

An alternative – which may work out cheaper in some countries – is to have a live-in nurse or companion.

HOSPITALISATION

If you are one of those people who like to give hospitals a wide berth, some words of reassurance. Standards of medical care are improving all around the world. I have met elderly expatriates living in Spain and elsewhere who have had complicated operations and are full of praise for the hospitals and the skill of the surgeons.

Yet difficulties remain. Soon after arriving in this country a refugee I know went into hospital to have a baby. She confessed to me that she found it a frightening experience, because she knew virtually no English and could not understand what was going on. On leaving hospital she resolved to accord the highest priority to learning the language.

If you are in a country where the national language is not English, your experience is likely to be similar. You cannot rely on having access to English-speaking hospital staff, but there are ways round the problem if you don't understand what is happening. Ask a friend to act as an interpreter and make sure you have a phrase book and a dictionary by your bedside.

How about returning to the UK for hospital treatment? This may be possible if you have a private insurance policy with an evacuation clause, but first you should check with the company. However if you have residence status and are under the state health scheme of your country of residence you will not be eligible for NHS treatment, unless you are returning to the UK for good.

INCOMPATIBILITY

In this book I have dwelt only fleetingly on the problems of people who go abroad to live with their children or other close relations. The reason for this is that they tend to be insulated from the problems faced by people who live independently.

However, these arrangements can turn sour. You may find that living with other people proves a strain, particularly if your lifestyle is quite different from theirs, and you feel that you are unable to lead your own life. There may be a touch of homesickness as well: you long for your circle of friends back home.

Clearly there is no merit in living in an atmosphere where you feel uncomfortable, but returning to the UK may seem an extreme step. The problem may stem from the fact that you have too much time on your hands, and can be solved if you try to make a social life for yourself. You might see if there are any clubs you can join, especially associations for the elderly.

If matters don't improve, don't degenerate into a moaning Minnie, but have a frank discussion with your relations. They are more likely to be relieved than angry if matters are brought out into the open. They are clearly concerned for your welfare, otherwise they would not have invited you to live with them, and it is important that you work out a solution together.

MARRIAGE PROBLEMS

Retirement is not without its problems. Wives who have got used to their husbands going out to work sometimes find that having a man about the house all day is too much of a good thing. If familiarity does not breed contempt, it can lead to the occasional bust-up.

Living in a completely new environment can put additional strains on individuals and consequently on their marriages. If a relationship was in a precarious state before the move abroad, a home in the sun is unlikely to revive it. On the contrary, it may precipitate the final break-up.

Ideally, before you come to any decision you should take advice. However, whereas in the UK there are a number of organisations (eg Relate) that can provide counselling and support, you cannot count on finding similar organisations abroad. Nor will you necessarily have your family close at hand to help resolve your differences.

You could ask around to see if there are any self-help groups, or you may be able to seek advice from a priest or someone from the local church. It may make sense for one or both of you to return to Britain for a time to reconsider the position. As mature people you should avoid coming to hasty decisions which could, among other things, have serious financial implications for you both, and try hard to resolve your differences.

SHORTAGE OF FUNDS

This can be a major problem. As I have mentioned elsewhere people do not normally get richer as they grow older: quite the reverse. If you are on a fixed pension you may find it buys less as the years go by. If a partner dies, there is further loss of income. Places where living was once cheap become popular and consequently much more expensive, so your money does not go as far as it once did. And unforeseen additional expenses may crop up.

If you are living in Britain there is plenty of assistance available from the welfare state. Once your savings fall below a certain amount supplementary benefits are payable, and there are other forms of financial help, too. However, you cannot count on such extensive support being available in other countries; even if it is, you may not be eligible for it.

Quite often people have a large amount of money tied up in property, and you could investigate the possibility of remortgaging the property to release some of the capital tied up in it. If your dwelling is now too large for your requirements you can sell it and go in for something smaller, or you could sell up completely and head back for Britain.

A case history
One elderly English lady living in Spain became extremely frail and was no longer capable of looking after herself. It was decided that the best solution was to send her back to Britain to stay in a residential home.

However, there was a dilemma: the lady was unable to pay home fees since her assets were tied up in her house in Spain which could not be sold because of the depressed housing market, and under Department of Social Security regulations she was not eligible for supplementary benefits because her capital was in excess of the upper limit for eligibility.

Eventually a compromise was reached. The DSS agreed to pay the residential home fees for the time being and would be reimbursed when her house in Spain was sold.

Nowadays in Britain the social service departments of local councils are responsible for paying residential home fees with the National Health Service paying a contribution to cover nursing fees.

THEFT

Crime is something that we have to learn to live with, alas, and the only thing we can really do is make life hard for the criminal. This means locks and security devices on our homes, particularly if we live in an isolated spot. If you are going to be away for any length of time it is sensible to alert your neighbours and perhaps the local police.

Make sure you know how to contact the police if your home is robbed or your car is broken into. If credit cards or cash are taken you should report the loss to the issuer immediately or you will be liable for any payments made on the account.

In southern Europe an increasing number of elderly people are buying homes on managed estates where security is better.

TROUBLE WITH THE AUTHORITIES

The fact that you are a foreign resident does not exclude you from the rights and obligations of other citizens of the country. It is your responsibility to find out what these responsibilities are. Ignorance of the law is no excuse.

For instance, you will probably be liable to pay some form of tax. There have been cases in Spain where foreigners have been fined or even had their assets seized because they haven't, and their names have appeared on the official debtor's list.

If you have a car, you may well have to put it through the equivalent of the MOT and tax it, otherwise you face a fine or arrest. If you get behind with your electricity or water payments you may find these utilities are cut off without warning.

If you are unable to resolve these problems satisfactorily by yourself, you should seek out someone who knows the ropes – your legal adviser, your local chaplain, the local expatriates' association or (if you are in serious trouble) the nearest British consul.

11

Returning Home

This chapter may seem out of place in a book dealing with retirement abroad. However, by no means everybody who retires to another country stays there indefinitely. Bereavement, deteriorating health, family considerations and dwindling savings are just four of the circumstances that may prompt you to return to the UK.

When you move abroad, the idea that one day you might return to the UK will be far from your mind. Indeed if you are the very picture of health the idea of your having to put up with the British climate again may sound down-right ridiculous. Yet any decision to return needs to be taken while you are still sufficiently robust to cope with the upheaval of moving. As Per Svensson puts it: 'Returning to Britain in your early seventies might be a wrench; returning to Britain in your early eighties could be a major problem.'[1]

It is therefore important to have contingency plans in order to ensure the operation goes as smoothly as possible. Much of the preparation will be obvious: the procedures will be similar to those you went through when you came. (See Chapter 7.)

BEFORE YOU GO

More haste less speed

Unless you are beset by an emergency and have no option other than to return to the UK in a hurry, it is advisable to indulge in a little forward planning, partly in order to minimise financial loss and make your homecoming a relatively smooth affair.

The first thing you need to consider is whether you will be returning home for good – or just for a few months. Some people have second thoughts when they arrive back in the UK and start to regret any decisions they have made in haste.

Assuming that you are leaving for good there will be plenty to sort out. For instance, if you own your current residence, you will probably want to dispose of it, unless you plan to keep it on as a holiday retreat. If you have no home in the UK, you will need to consider where you are going to live and start to make arrangements. There may be dependents or pets to be considered.

However, one of your first considerations will be to make sure that your financial affairs are in order and you must look into the tax implications of any move.

UK tax considerations

Your return to the UK – even if it is only temporary – could be a bonanza for the Inland Revenue, unless you exercise due care. You should bear in mind that you become subject to UK tax if

- you move back to the UK on a permanent basis;
- you stay in the UK for 183 days or more in one year;
- you visit the UK and have accommodation available for your use (see Chapter 6);
- you visit the UK regularly and after four tax years your visits average 91 days or more per tax year.

If you return prematurely you might even have to pay tax arrears. This would happen, for instance, if

- you are treated as a resident from the year in which you decided to make regular visits averaging 91 days;
- you have only provisional non-residential status in the eyes of the Inland Revenue and return within three years of your departure from the UK. This could mean you are liable for three years' tax.

This is why it makes sense to check with a financial adviser before you return. Although a good adviser may not be able to remove your tax liability entirely, he should be able to suggest ways of lessening it.

One idea might be for you to dispose of assets that have appreciated in value before you move back to the UK. In certain cases this may have to be done in the tax year before you move back.

Once you are back in the UK you need to re-establish contact with the Inland Revenue.

Foreign tax considerations

It is not only your liability to UK tax that you need to investigate. If you have had residential status in your country of abode you will need to find out what taxes you have to pay there. If, for instance, you sell your property at a profit you may be liable for capital gains tax.

Before you leave it is vital to put your tax affairs in order. You may be obliged to appoint a fiscal representative to take responsibility for any payments that are due – and this applies to local taxes, too.

SELLING UP

Preliminaries

If you own a property you need to dispose of it. If you do not have a buyer lined up you have a choice of methods:

- you engage someone to sell it for you – an estate agent, solicitor or notary; – or
- you sell it yourself.

Whichever way you choose to sell it you have first to decide on the following:

The asking price

This will depend very much on the price of similar properties in the area, the state of the property market and who is likely to buy. In some areas (eg rural France) your best bet will be another expatriate; in others (eg Switzerland) there may be restrictions on selling to someone who is not a national of the country.

What to include in the sale

For example, curtains, furniture, kitchen equipment. This will depend very much on what you wish to take home with you, bearing in mind removal costs. If some of the furniture is valuable, you will doubtless want to take it away with you or else sell it separately from the house, but there will be less of a case for shipping the curtains and the kitchen stove back home.

If you engage a local estate agent to handle the sale, make sure that he is reputable and is legally entitled to practise. In several continental countries estate agents have to be licensed. Alternatively you could appoint an agent in the UK or ask a private individual to sell on your behalf. In the latter case you may need to give the person power of attorney in some countries using a notary or solicitor.

Your property description

Sooner or later a description of your house will be drawn up and it is advisable to check the details, since these may well feature in any sale contract. The description should include

- the address
- general description of the property and its setting
- a detailed description of each room (dimensions, electric points, heating, built-in cupboards, etc)
- description of the garden and any outbuildings
- the price
- local taxes payable.

Using an estate agent

Selling through a reputable agent takes a good deal of the responsibility off your shoulders. He will value the property and judge how best to sell the house. He will publicise the sale, arrange for potential buyers to view the property, negotiate a price, check the buyer's financial status and perhaps even arrange a mortgage for him/her so that the sale proceeds smoothly.

It is wise to enquire before you engage him how much his services will cost, and read the small print of any form you sign. Points to note are:

- *sole agency status*: if you entrust the sale to one agent, check if you have to pay a commission even if you make a private sale;

- *fixed period*: the agent should be given a fixed period in which to effect a sale, after which the contract lapses or is negotiable;

- *commission*: this is normally a percentage of the sale price. Note that the commissions for selling a property abroad are generally higher than in the UK, particularly if two agents in different countries are involved.

In some areas it is quite customary for notaries and solicitors to act as intermediaries for the vendor, as is the case in Scotland.

Handling the sale yourself
In order to cut out the middleman you may decide to sell the house yourself, though this can involve considerable effort. You will need to proceed along the following lines.

- Draft an advertisement which includes the following information:
  - type of property
  - location
  - number of bedrooms
  - heating system
  - garden
  - other desirable amenities
  - freehold or leasehold
  - asking price
  - contact telephone number or address – this would really need to be a UK address or number if you expect a buyer from the UK.

  It is a good idea to include a photograph of the property.

- Place the advertisement with suitable newspapers (eg *Dalton's Weekly, Exchange & Mart*), local expatriate papers and specialist foreign property magazines (see bibliography in Appendix D). Advertising rates for UK national newspapers tend to be quite high, so you should think twice before advertising with these – or keep your advertisement brief.

In some countries it is customary to put up a For Sale notice outside a property.

Legal arrangements

Having already bought a property in the country you will doubtless be an expert by now on the legal aspects of buying and selling a house. You are strongly advised to employ a legal adviser to act on your behalf, since if any mistakes are made in the process you could be liable to compensate the buyer.

In some countries it is the responsibility of the vendor to notify the authorities of any transfer of ownership of the property.

Repatriating the proceeds of your sale

If you are planning to buy a home in the UK on the proceeds from the sale of your current home, bear in mind that you may have less to spend than you expect because of liability to capital gains tax – either in the UK or in your country of residence. In France you may have to pay VAT if the property is less than five years old.

In some countries the notary keeps back some of the proceeds from the sale to pay taxes and any other liabilities. You will receive the balance in due course.

Note that there could be problems in repatriating the proceeds. In Cyprus, for instance, you can remit the equivalent of the purchase price, but any profit you make on the transaction has to be taken out over a period of years.

Pets

Do not forget that restrictions exist on the movement of animals from country to country, even pets. However, under the Pet Travel Scheme (PETS) you can bring dogs and cats into the UK from most western European countries (including Malta and Greece) without having to place them in quarantine for six months. However you need to ensure that any animal has been:

- fitted with a microchip
- vaccinated against rabies
- blood tested to show it is protected against rabies (six months prior to travel)
- issued with an official PETS certificate
- treated against tapeworm and ticks and certificated (1–2 days before travel).

It must also travel to Britain by an authorised route. Vets, pet travel specialists and British consulates should be able to advice you on all the requirements. Pets travelling from certain overseas countries may also qualify for the Pets Travel Scheme, but to make sure you should either consult the DEFRA website or telephone the PETS helpline. (Details in Appendix C: Government Departments.) In many cases, however, quarantine is unavoidable, though in some instances it may not stretch to the full six months.

Social Security
It is vital to inform the social security authorities in your country of residence and the Benefits Agency Overseas Branch of your movements, preferably well in advance of your departure. This will ensure that your pension payments are not interrupted and are sent to the right place. When you arrive back, the local social security office will advise you of what benefits, if any, are due to you.

WHEN YOU ARRIVE IN THE UK

Registration with a doctor
If you are planning to stay in the UK for good – or for an extended period – and wish to be treated on the NHS you need to register with a general practitioner. It is just a matter of finding one who is prepared to take you on and signing a form. The local Family Practitioners' Committee will then get in touch with you and issue you with a medical

card. If you can remember your old NHS number, the process can be speeded up.

Should you have problems in finding a doctor who will take you on his or her list, consult the Family Practitioners' Committee listed in the local telephone directory.

If your stay is going to be a short one (a matter of months) you will be eligible for emergency treatment provided there is a social security treaty with the country you have just come from. You need not register with a doctor, but if you need to consult one you will be required to fill in a special form.

Accommodation in the UK

Ideally you need to plan this matter well in advance. This is particularly true if you have property in the UK which is rented out, and you need to give your tenants notice. Unfortunately in such an instance you cannot always rely on your house being vacant when you want it: I know of instances where a court order had to be issued in order to remove tenants.

If you have no residence in the UK you have a choice:

- Stay with friends and relations. Normally this would be a temporary expedient until something else turns up.

- Find rented accommodation. The best place to look is in local newspapers or contact a letting agent. If this is a temporary expedient you could rent a holiday home. These are often available at cheap rates during the off-season. Among the companies specialising in this field is English Country Cottages.

- Purchase a new home. This is usually a lengthy undertaking unless you have already set things in motion while you were abroad, and you may not be able to move in immediately. There may also be problems in financing the purchase if you have not yet sold your property abroad. Banks and building societies are often reluctant to offer mortgages backed by foreign assets, but you could explore ways of raising the finance with a mortgage broker.

- If you feel you are going to need some form of sheltered accommodation there are a number of sources of information. Saga, for instance publishes a register of purpose-built retirement housing, and the bi-monthly magazine *Retirement Homes & Finance* has an index of current retirement property developments.

- Enter a residential home. Rest homes and nursing homes are a more expensive option (currently between £350 and £500 per week). Local authorities can provide a list of homes in their particular areas, Age Concern publishes a fact sheet on residential homes, and independent advisers, such as Grace Consulting; can suggest homes that will match your requirements.

Your will

This will need to be altered to reflect changed circumstances. If you do not intend to return to the country where you have been living you will need to investigate what action is necessary with respect to your foreign will.

Financial matters

It is advisable to see your financial adviser as early as possible to review your financial strategy, particularly in the light of your changed tax circumstances. Insurances may also need to be reviewed.

Reverse culture shock

This is a problem a number of expatriates face when they arrive back on British shores, particularly those who have been living in a milder climate. You may miss the sunshine, the warmth, the inexpensive booze, the camaraderie, the relaxed lifestyle.

For a little while you will feel like a fish out of water, and it will take time to adapt. The Britain you knew might have changed out of all recognition. People's tastes and behaviour may also have changed, and this can sometimes give rise to irritation.

However, things will come right in time. Take care of

your health and keep active, and if everyone you used to know seems to have moved on, join a few clubs and make new friends just as you did when you first settled abroad.

REFERENCE

1. Svensson, Per: *Buying & Selling Your Home in Spain* (Longman).

12

Alternatives to Retiring Abroad

The purpose of this book is not to sell the idea that retiring abroad is a good thing. Instead it has sought to help you weigh up the implications and come to an informed decision and point you in the right direction if you decide to take the plunge.

However, after giving the matter serious consideration you may decide to proceed no further. This is not necessarily because you have no taste for adventure or a place in the sun, but because of a combination of other factors.

REASONS FOR NOT RETIRING ABROAD

Emotional ties
If you have strong roots in your local community it may come as an enormous wrench to pull up these roots and plant them elsewhere. Emotional ties are important, particularly as you grow older, and a sunny clime is no compensation for what you leave behind. Your friends and relations, the skittles matches at your local pub, WEA courses, whist drives and church socials may be essential features of your life which you will miss.

Failing health
If your health is poor or you are disabled, the strain and stress of moving may prove more than you can bear. Even if the climate of the country you have in mind is healthier than that of the UK, it is reassuring to know that if your health breaks down in Britain you will be treated by people you know in conditions with which you are familiar and – if

you are a National Health Service patient – free (or almost free) of charge.

Insufficient finance

You need to bear in mind that although housing may seem cheaper in many foreign countries your actual living expenses could turn out to be higher than in the UK in the long run. Even if you have a reasonable pension, this may not be adequate to cope with unforeseen eventualities, and some cash in reserve is a must.

Difficulty in selling your house in the UK

Quite often the purchase of a property abroad is dependent on the sale of one's home in the UK. In a buoyant house market this presents few problems, but if the market is flat, you may consider it too risky to proceed with the acquisition of a property overseas.

Second thoughts about retirement

The veteran novelist Mary Wesley once said that she considered retirement to be a form of suicide. There must be many retired people who share her view and secretly long to be actively employed. There are, alas, very few job opportunities for retired expatriates, and some countries discourage you from working.

A case history

An entrepreneur from the North East decided to move to Spain and appoint a manager to run his business. However, it was not long before he became bored with life in the sun and having no work to do. When the factory began to go through a bad patch, he decided to return to the UK and take the helm again, and was very happy to do so. Living abroad had not worked for him.

THE ALTERNATIVES

When all is said and done, there is a good case to be made

for staying put and taking extended holidays. The great thing about being retired is that you can take holidays in the off-peak seasons which usually coincide with school terms. At this time of year holiday resorts are quieter and often much nicer, and charges are much, much lower. Or you might even find some work assignments to do abroad.

Let's look at these suggestions in greater detail.

Renting accommodation

How about spending one, two or three months abroad? In the off-season holiday home rental charges fall dramatically, as do charter air fares, and the longer you stay the cheaper it gets. A number of the established tour operators feature long-stay holidays in self-catering accommodation in their brochures, with prices as low as £70 week for a long stay.

If you do not want to be 'packaged', look in the classified ad columns in holiday magazines such as *Private Villas*, or in newspapers, including the weekly *Exchange and Mart*, for accommodation offers placed by individual owners. Some estate agents also handle lettings as a service to their clients.

You may be worried about leaving your home in the UK vacant while you are abroad, and your insurance company may also have qualms. If you are unable to find a friend or relation to keep an eye on it or live in it, you should consider engaging the services of a 'house-minding' agency such as Housewatch, Homesitters or Animal Aunts.

Home exchanges

A cheaper alternative is to exchange your home with someone else for a period. You may already know someone – a pen friend, perhaps – who would welcome a chance to live in your house or flat and let you live in theirs rent-free. If not, you could try an agency which will either match your requirements with those of a houseowner abroad or else circulate details of your home in a home exchange directory. Among the agencies offering such a service are Intervac Home Exchange, which pioneered the concept and has members in 50 countries, Home Base Holidays and Homelink International.

Living in a hotel

During the British winter it is possible to stay very cheaply in hotels in Spain, Portugal, Malta, Cyprus, Tunisia and Florida. The reason for this is that in the off-season establishments prefer to have some clients rather than none at all just to pay their overheads and keep their staff employed. Some hotels arrange a social programme for long-stay visitors, including painting, keep-fit and cookery classes.

A number of the leading travel operators offer winter sun holidays (eg Saga, Cosmos Golden Times, Thomson Young in Heart). Among the bargains I have noticed are three-month stays in leading holiday resorts for well under £2,000, including full board and air travel. Prices like this compare very favourably with living at home in the UK during the winter months when heating costs soar.

Cruises and extended tours

Many people regard a cruise as the ultimate holiday, but they are essentially for people with plenty of time and cash. Among the leading operators in the field are Cunard and Fred Olsen. If you are more adventurous you might consider a trip on a cargo boat which could take several weeks.

Alternatively how about a trip round Europe or even further afield by car? This offers you considerable flexibility, especially if you go outside the main holiday season. There is normally no need to book your accommodation in advance, although there are various holiday companies that can suggest itineraries and organise accommodation on the way for you.

You need to acquire a good guide book and an up-to-date hotel list from the relevant national tourist offices in the UK before you go. Both the AA and RAC can help you with your travel arrangements including ferry, insurance and accommodation.

Rail travel is another good way to get about, particularly within Europe where the rail systems are normally very efficient. You can obtain reductions of up to 50% on rail tickets in Europe if you have a Senior Railcard. If you want to do a lot of travelling over a short time a senior citizen's Rail-Europe Card may prove more appropriate.

For a more detailed exploration of holiday opportunities *The Good Non-Retirement Guide* is recommended.

A holiday home

Your own property
If you fancy the idea of extended stays abroad but still want to maintain a UK base you might consider buying a holiday property abroad. When you are not using it you may be able to let it to friends and relations or else use the services of a letting agency. A number of estate agents and holiday firms offer this service.

It is increasingly common for people to acquire a holiday home several years before they retire with the idea that they might settle down there eventually. There is a great deal of merit in such an idea: you have a chance to get to know the area thoroughly and are in a better position to judge whether you would really feel at home as a permanent resident. However, you have to bear in mind that in certain countries, such as the USA, because of immigration restrictions, it may be impossible to take up residence for the whole year round.

Purchasing a holiday property normally entails going through the same procedures as buying a permanent home (see Chapter 4). If it is on a holiday estate there is often a management company to keep an eye on the property for you during your absences.

You should bear in mind that although you are not a full-time resident you will probably be liable for taxes of one sort or another, notably local taxes and possibly a tax on letting income. In some countries (eg Spain) you may also have to appoint someone within the country to be responsible for your tax affairs, sometimes known as a fiscal representative.

Shared ownership
If your finances do not stretch to buying a complete

property abroad, shared ownership is a sensible compromise. You find two or three other individuals or families to share the cost with you (purchase price and upkeep), and have the use of the property for three or four months of the year – a kind of DIY time-share system.

With such an arrangement it is sensible to draw up a legal agreement which defines the rights and responsibilities of the partners. Particular attention needs to be paid to:

- arrangements for allocating periods of the year when a particular partner and his family can occupy the house;

- arrangements for buying out a partner if he decides to withdraw;

- arrangements for contributing to the cost of maintenance, taxes and other bills;

- restrictions on ownership (eg with regard to the ownership of pets).

Setting up a shared ownership scheme yourself can lead to complications. For instance, a prospective partner may back out at the last moment and there could be problems in registering and transferring ownership. In order to simplify matters a number of agents and developers can arrange so-called Four Owners Schemes for you.

David Scott International, for instance, operates a scheme in which the co-owners are shareholders in a company registered in London which takes care of all the legal charges and taxes. Each co-owner has a use agreement with the company to regulate his occupation, rights and obligations. In this way the co-owners have full and direct security of ownership, and shares may be sold and transferred without incurring expensive legal charges or taxes.

Time sharing
The idea behind time shares is that you buy a share in a property which allows you to use it for a set period every

year (typically a week or a fortnight) for an agreed term or in perpetuity. The amount you pay depends very much on the time of year you spend there: off-season rates could be as much as a third lower than high season rates.

Although you have a share in a particular property you may be able to swap it for a holiday in another property. This is possible if your time-share company is affiliated to a time-share exchange organisation as most of them are.

Time shares should not be regarded as an investment which will appreciate over a period of time. The cost of marketing time-share properties is high and has to be recouped in the prices charged, so it is debatable whether a time share represents value for money.

Although claims are made that you will never have to pay for holiday accommodation again, most share properties have annual service charges to cover such items as maintenance, repairs, decoration, local taxes, maid service and management, so in fact you do. Such charges have a tendency to rise.

People have become wary of time-share deals because of the dubious selling techniques employed by some time-share companies (eg offering lavish prizes to people who attend their presentations and then putting pressure on them to buy). The Timeshare Consumers Association is trying to combat these practices. It is sensible to check with them the credentials of any company offering you a time share. The Department of Trade and Industry publishes a free leaflet on timesharing obtainable from its consumer leaflets department which is essential reading.

Property co-operative
An alternative to buying a specific time-share property is to join a property co-operative. The UK leader in this field is the Villa Owners Club Ltd which has devised the Holiday Property Bond.

This is a life assurance bond where each investor owns a financial interest in a range of holiday properties which he can use rent-free for holidays. The funds are also invested in securities which produce income to help offset management and maintenance charges. Like any bond it is encashable and the value can rise and fall. However, your stay will not be completely cost-free as all holidays are subject to a user charge covering electricity, laundry, maintenance, maid service, etc.

Unlike time-share operations you are not committed to staying at the same property for the same period each year, but can spend your holiday at any of the 550 plus properties the Club owns at locations in Spain, France, Greece, Italy, Portugal, Cyprus, Austria and Britain. The scheme has been in operation for more than twenty years, and its members elect representatives to the Property Advisory Committee.

A JOB ABROAD

Not everybody relishes the prospect of a life of leisure, and this is especially true of those who have taken early retirement. If the idea of working abroad for a limited time appeals to you, why not investigate? Age often proves to be less of a handicap when you apply for an overseas job than it is if you look for UK-based employment. Some countries, for instance, value maturity and experience.

It is advantageous if you can point to some overseas experience on your CV, but this is not obligatory. I remember coming across a cotton spinning expert well into his sixties working for the Department for International Development in Thailand. I later met an elderly gentleman directing a project for the Save the Children Fund. More recently there have been stories of retired teachers going off to India to impart their knowledge under the auspices of Teaching and Projects Abroad.

Where do you look for such jobs? Rather than look through the job ads and apply for specific posts, you will find it more fruitful to adopt a speculative approach and forward your details to organisations which you feel might be able to use your talents. Pass on the word to your business and professional contacts that you are interested in going off on a foreign assignment.

Few of the jobs in the voluntary sector are well paid. Indeed, you may receive only board and lodging and have to make a financial contribution yourself. However, the point of the exercise is not to make a profit, but to do something which is interesting and challenging.

Self-employment is another option, but you will need to make sure first that there is a ready market for your services and that you have the necessary permission to practise your trade or profession.

A useful source of information is the ecumenical organisation Christians Abroad which publishes a leaflet entitled *A Place for You Overseas – the Over-50s* and a monthly bulletin of overseas vacancies with voluntary and missionary organisations. People with professional, technical or management skills who are interested in voluntary assignments lasting weeks rather than months or years should get in touch with British Executive Service Overseas, a development charity which sends senior managers mainly to Third World countries and Eastern Europe.

You will find a much fuller discussion of job possibilities in foreign countries in other books in the How To series, notably *Getting a Job Abroad, Teaching Abroad, Getting a Job in America, Getting a Job in Australia, Getting a Job in Europe* and *Getting a Job in France.* Vacation Work publishes *The Directory of Jobs and Careers Abroad, The International Directory of Voluntary Work* and other useful handbooks.

Vacancies are advertised in the national press and international job papers such as *Nexus* and *Overseas Jobs Express* (see Bibliography).

A FINAL WORD

With increased longevity it is possible that your retirement could be of longer duration than your working career. That is why it makes good sense to regard retirement not as the evening of your life, but rather as the afternoon, and plan accordingly. By keeping active and developing new interests you will begin to enjoy life to the full, freed from many of the worries of your earlier years. The alternative is to merely sit back and relax, which becomes a drag after a short while.

In this book I have attempted to show you how to make the most of your retirement either by opting to live abroad permanently in a more congenial clime or to spend several months of the year in foreign parts. Either of these options could bring an extra dimension to your life, so I hope that you will approach my suggestions with an open mind.

The decision is yours. Whatever you decide, let me take this opportunity to wish you a long and enjoyable retirement!

Appendix A
Retirement Locations in Europe

COVERAGE

Andorra	Channel Islands	Greece	Malta & Gozo
Austria	Cyprus	Irish Republic	Portugal
Azores	France	Isle of Man	Spain
Balearic Islands	Germany	Italy	Switzerland
Canary Islands	Gibraltar	Madeira	Turkey

ANDORRA

Population: 80,000   Area: 175 sq miles (453 sq km)
International dialling code: 00 376
A mountainous country situated 3,000 feet above sea level in the Pyrenees between France and Spain. Four out of five residents are non-Andorrans attracted partly by the absence of taxation.

Representation in the UK
Andorran Delegation: 63 Westover Road, London SW18 2RF. Tel: (020) 8874 4806.

Nearest UK representation to Andorra
Consulate: Edificia Torre de Barcelona, Avenida Diagonal 477, 08036 Barcelona. Tel: 00 34 96 419 9044.

Immigration regulations
Once you own a property in Andorra you can apply for residence. You will need a bank reference to show you have sufficient funds to live on.

Property purchase
Must be done through a notary. There is a limit on the amount of land you can buy.

Tax
There is no income tax, capital gains tax or VAT liability. No double taxation agreement with UK.

Health insurance
There is a state health scheme which you will be able to join with good clinics and hospitals. The health service pays two-thirds of the medical bills. There is no social security agreement between the UK and Andorra.

Languages
Catalan, Spanish, French

Currency
French and Spanish

Other
Cars imported into Andorra must be under three years old. New cars are considerably cheaper in Andorra than in the UK.

AUSTRIA

Population: 8 million   Area: 32,374 sq miles (83,849 sq km)
International dialling code: 00 43
While it is a popular tourist destination, Austria has not attracted many British retirees. The southern areas of the country (notably Carinthia) have the mildest winters, but British buyers tend to go for the Tirol.

Austrian representation in UK
Embassy: 18 Belgrave Mews West, London SW1X 8HU.
   Tel: (020) 7235 3731.
Tourist Office: PO Box 2363, London W1R 0AL.

Tel: (020) 7269 0461.

British representation in Austria

Embassy: Jauresgasse 10–12, A-1030 Vienna. Tel: 00 43 1 713 1575.
Consulates: Bundesstrasse 110, A-6923 Lauterach-Bregenz.
Schmiedgasse 8-12, A-8000 Graz.
Matthias Schmidstrasse 12, A-6021 Innsbruck.
Alter Markt 4, A-5020 Salzburg.

Immigration

Austria is now a member of the European Union so UK citizens do not need a visa to enter the country.

Tax

Double taxation agreement with UK.

Social security

Agreement with the UK (Ref leaflet SA25). For information about Austrian scheme: Hauptverband der Österreichischen Sozialversicherungsträger, Kundmanngasse 21, Postfach 600, A-1030 Wien or local social insurance offices (Krankenkasse).

UK state pension

Payable at rate prevailing in the UK.

AZORES

Population: 250,000   Area: 933 sq miles
International dialling code: 00 351
A group of nine Portuguese islands several hundred miles to the west of Portugal.

British representation

Consulate: Largo Vasco Bensaúde 13, 9500 Pont Delgada (Azores).
Tel: 00 351 296 22201.

See Portugal entry for further details.

BALEARIC ISLANDS

Population: 760,000   Area: 1,935 sq miles
International dialling code: 00 34
An archipelago of 11 islands off the east coast of Spain, the largest being Mallorca, Menorca, Ibiza and Formentera. Part of Spain.

British consulates
Plaza Mayor 3D, 07002 Palma de Mallorca. Tel: 00 34 971 712445.
Avda Isidoro Macabich 45-1°, Apdo 307, 07800 Ibiza. Tel: 00 34 971 301818.
Torret 28, San Luis, Menorca. Tel: 00 34 971 151536.

See Spain entry for further details.

CANARY ISLANDS

Population: 1.6 million   Area: 2,807 sq miles
International dialling code: 00 34
Archipelago of seven Spanish islands to the west of Morocco with a much warmer climate than Europe. They comprise two provinces: Las Palmas (Gran Canaria, Fuerteventura, Lanzarote) and Santa Cruz de Tenerife (Tenerife, La Palma, Gomera, Hierro).

British consulates
Edificio Cataluna, C/Luis Morote 6, 35007 Las Palmas, Grand Canary. Tel: 00 34 928 262508.
Plaza Weyler 8-1°, 38003 Santa Cruz de Tenerife. Tel: 00 34 922 286863.
Calle Rubicón No 7, Arrecife, Lanzarote. Tel: 00 34 928 815928.

Reference
Freedom for Sale Magazine. Tel: 00 34 928 835411.
  Website: www.freedom4sale.com.

For further information see Spain entry.

CHANNEL ISLANDS
Population: 145,000   Area: 75 sq miles (195 sq km)
We may not regard these islands as foreign soil, but there are sufficient differences to merit inclusion in a book of this nature. For instance, they have complete autonomy in domestic and fiscal matters. Generally speaking properties for outsiders are expensive.

Useful addresses
States Offices, Royal Square, St Helier, Jersey.
States Offices, St Peter Port, Guernsey.

Immigration
Jersey's highly restrictive immigration policy virtually rules it out as a retirement option. Normally you cannot buy property in your own name until you have resided on the island for at least 20 years.

Guernsey operates a system of 'open market' properties – some 10% of the total and which anyone can buy. These are usually the more expensive properties. The more reasonably priced 'local market' properties can only be occupied by local residents and those licensed to come to the island to take up employment.

The situation in Alderney, part of the Bailiwick of Guernsey, is more promising.

Tax
There is a double taxation agreement with the UK. Taxation is low.

Social security
There is a reciprocal agreement with the UK. For information on the social security scheme in Jersey contact: The States of Jersey Social Security Department, Philip Le Feuvre House, La Motte Street, St Helier, Jersey. For the other islands contact: States Insurance Authority, Edward T Wheadon House, Le Truchot, St Peter Port, Guernsey.

CYPRUS

Population: 800,000   Area: 3,572 sq miles (9,251 sq km)
International dialling code: 00 357 (Republic of Cyprus); 00
905 (Northern Cyprus)
The third largest island in the Mediterranean, Cyprus with its
climate, relatively low cost of living and the widespread use
of English has attracted a number of retirees, and some
60,000 Britons now have homes (or second homes) here.
However, house prices are currently rising. Note that Cyprus
is a divided island.

The northern part – roughly a third of the island – is
designated the Turkish Republic of Northern Cyprus and is
less developed. Not all of the information that follows is
necessarily applicable to Northern Cyprus.

Cypriot representation in the UK
High Commission: 93 Park Street, London W1Y 4ET.
    Tel: (020) 7499 8272.
Turkish Republic of Northern Cyprus: 29 Bedford Square,
    London WC1B 3EG. Tel: (020) 7631 1920.

UK representation in Cyprus (Republic)
British High Commission: Alexander Pallis Street, PO Box
    1978, Nicosia. Tel: 00 357 2 273131.

Property restrictions
At one time foreigners were allowed to own most kinds of
property so long as it did not extend to more than two-thirds
of an acre. Now rules regarding property ownership by
foreigners are being relaxed as Cyprus prepares for full
membership of the European Union in 2003.

Property purchase
This is fairly straightforward as Cypriot law is based on
English law. It is advisable to employ a lawyer, though most
people do not. When a contract is signed it is submitted to
the Land Registry (submission for specific performance).
Buying costs, including registration and transfer tax, legal

fees and stamp duty, add 8 to 9% to the purchase price. New property often carries a six-month guarantee. To gain freehold title non-Cypriots need to show that the property has been paid for in foreign currency and permission has been granted by the Council of Ministers.

Property sales
Capital gains tax currently stands at 20%.

Residence
You need to demonstrate that you have sufficient income to maintain yourself. Ownership of immovable property will enable you to gain residential status. However, a condition of your residence permit may be that you are not permitted to work.

Social security
Agreement with the UK (Ref leaflet SA12). There is a good standard of public and private medical care. For information on the Cyprus scheme contact: Department of Social Insurance, 7 Byron Avenue, Nicosia, Cyprus.

Tax
Income tax is payable on income derived from Cyprus. UK pensions are therefore exempt. Immovable property tax is 0.15% per annum. There is a double taxation agreement with the UK.

Cost of living
Lower than UK, but house prices are now rising sharply, especially around Limassol, Larnaca and Paphos.

UK state pension
Payable at rate prevailing in the UK.

Reference
Buying a Home in Greece and Cyprus (Survival Books).
Cyprus Weekly, PO Box 1992, 216 Mitsis 3 Building, Archbishop Makarios Avenue, Nicosia. Tel: 00 357 2 441433.

FRANCE

Population: 59 million   Area: 211,000 sq miles (547,026 sq km)
International dialling code: 00 33
One of the largest countries in Europe in terms of area,
France with its varied regions has attracted large numbers of
British settlers in recent years. Rural locations in the
Dordogne area and NW France have been especially
popular. Many areas have retirement homes catering for
elderly French people, but there are sheltered housing
developments for expatriates on the Côte d'Azur. An ability
to speak French is essential to get to grips with the red tape
and to socialise effectively with the locals.

French representation in the UK
Embassy: 58 Knightsbridge, London SW1 7JT. Tel: (020)
    7201 1000.
Consulate: 21 Cromwell Road, London SW7 2EN. Tel: (020)
    7581 5292. Visa section: PO Box 57, 6A Cromwell Place,
    London SW7 2EW. Tel: (020) 7823 9555.
Tourist Office: 178 Piccadilly, London W1V 0AL. Tel: (020)
    7491 7622.

British representation in France
Embassy: 105–109 rue de Faubourg St Honoré, 75008 Paris.
    Tel: 00 33 1 4451 3100.
Consulates: 35 boulevard du President Wilson, 33073
    Bordeaux. Tel: 00 33 5 5722 2110.
    20 rue du Havre, 62100 Calais. Tel: 00 33 3 2196 3376.
    7 boulevard Tauzin, 64200 Biarritz. Tel: 00 33 5 5924 2140.
    8 boulevard des Marechaux, 35800 Dinard. Tel: 00 33 2
    9946 2664.
    24 rue Childebert, 69002 Lyon. Tel: 00 33 4 7277 8170.
    24 avenue du Prado, 13006 Marseille. Tel: 00 33 4 9115
    7210.
    Le Palace, Entrée A, 8 rue Alphonse Karr, 06000 Nice.
    Tel: 00 33 4 9382 3204.

Other useful addresses

Fédération Nationale des Agents Immobiliers, 129 rue du
Faubourg St Honoré, 75008 Paris. Tel: 00 33 1 4429 7700.
(Federation of Estate Agents)

Conseil Supérieur du Notariat, 31 rue du Général Foy, 75008
Paris. Tel: 00 33 1 4293 00 33 695.

Immigration procedures

Before the end of your first three months in France you need
to apply to the Préfecture for a *carte de séjour*. Long-stay
visas are no longer obligatory for retired people.

Social security

Agreement with the UK (Ref leaflet SA29) under EC
regulations (see Chapter 4). For treatment under the French
health scheme you must check that the doctor or dentist is
'conventionné'. Further information from local Caisse
Primaire d'Assurance-Maladie which will refund proportion
of cost of treatment. Only a proportion of the cost of
treatment is refunded, so people often take out private
medical insurance from *mutuelles*.

Tax

Double taxation agreement with the UK. Indirect taxation is
heavier than in the UK. The Fiscal Attaché at the French
Embassy can provide you with details. Two local taxes
payable: the *taxe foncière* by owner, *taxe d'habitation* by
occupant. If letting property tenants pay percentage of rent
agreed in tax.

House purchase

A notary (*notaire*) is a public official who handles the
conveyancing and other legal formalities and normally acts
for both vendor and purchaser, although each party may
appoint an independent notary to assist them at no extra
cost. A notary may also operate as an estate agent as many
lawyers in Scotland do.

The house agent (*agent immobilier*) brings together vendor and purchaser as in the UK. He may be given power of attorney for the buyer with power to execute the final conveyance deed at the notary's office.

An architect may be employed to conduct a house survey. Surveys are not all that common in France, but that could well change in the future. It is clearly in your interest to employ one, especially in the case of an older property.

House buying procedures differ from those in the UK.

1. The preliminary sale contract is drawn up, preferably by a notary, but the house agent may also do it, and a deposit of around 10% is made. This may be either:
   - a *promesse unilatérale de vente* (which is an option excercisable only on the terms stated)
   - or a *compromis de vente/promesse de vente* (which is a more legally binding agreement to buy on the terms stated).

   In either case if you decide not to go ahead with the purchase you are likely to lose your deposit.
2. The notary carries out various searches and, if the conditions stipulated in the first contract are satisfied, he will draw up the deed of sale (*acte authentique de vente*). This has to be signed by both vendor and buyer in his presence, and then registered in the land registry. He retains the deed and provides you with a copy.

Typical costs: notarial fees (up to 5% of purchase price plus VAT, more if you require advice outside the normal parameters of house purchase); estate agent's fees (up to 4%); land registry fees (5%); stamp duty (£100 plus); translations; VAT on properties less than five years old. Mortgages attract an additional notary's fee.

If you are buying a new property the process is as follows:

1. Reservation contract: a deposit of up to 5% is paid.
2. Legal completion: *acte de vente*, abridged specifications, payment of notary, second stage of payment.
3. Physical completion. Inspection by architect. Final payment.

Magazines

Everything France, The Barn, Ladycross Farm, Hollow Lane, Dormansland, Surrey RH7 6PB. Tel: (01342) 871727.

France (quarterly), Beautiful Magazines, Dorma House, The Square, Stow on the Wold, Glos GL51 1BN. Tel: (01451) 833200.

Living France, The Picture House, 79 High Street, Olney, Bucks MK46 4EF. Tel: (01234) 713203. Website: www.livingfrance.com.

Focus on France (Outbound Publishers).

French Property News, 6 Burgess Mews, London SW19 1UF. Tel: (020) 08543 9868. Website: www.french-property-news.com

Reference books

Blackstone Franks Guide to Living in France (Blackstone Franks).

Buying and Restoring Old Property in France, David Everett (Robert Hale).

Buying and Selling Your Home in France, Henry Dyson (Sweet & Maxwell).

Buying Residential Property in France, French Chamber of Commerce, 197 Knightsbridge, London SW7 1RB. Tel: (020) 7225 5250.

Buying a Home in France, David Hampshire (Survival Guides).

Buying a Property in France, Philip Jones (ed) (Kogan Page).

Live and Work in France, Victoria Pybus (Vacation Work).

Living and Working in France, Genevieve Brame (Kogan Page).

Living and Working in France (Survival Guides).

Living and Working in Paris, Alan Hart (How To Books).

A Guide to Buying Property in France (Bennett & Co, Wilmslow).

How to Rent and Buy a Property in France, Clive Kristen (How To Books).

Living as a British Expatriate in France (French Chamber of Commerce).

Some of My Best Friends are French, Colin Corder (Shelf Publishers. Tel: (01438) 820059).
Buying a Property in France, Philip Jones (Kogan Page).
Taxation in France, Charles Parkinson (PKF, Guernsey).

GERMANY

Population: 78 million   Area: 137,750 sq miles (354,755 sq km)
International dialling code: 00 49
Although the industrial powerhouse of Europe may not seem the obvious place to retire to, thousands of British pensioners do live there. The south of the country is very attractive, but the cost of living is less so.

German representation in the UK
Embassy: 23 Belgrave Square, London SW1X 8PZ. Tel: (020) 7824 1300. Website: www.german-embassy.org.uk.
Tourist Office: 61 Conduit Street, London W1R 0EN. Tel: (020) 7734 2600.

UK representation in Germany
British Embassy:
    Argelanderstrasse 108a, 53115 Bonn.
    Wilhelmstrasse 70, 10117 Berlin.
Consulates in Frankfurt, Hamburg, Hanover, Kiel, Munich, Nuremberg and Stuttgart.

Immigration procedures
EC regulations apply. Within three months of your arrival you should register with the Einwohnermeldeamt or the Ausländerbehörde of the local council to obtain a residence permit (*Aufenthaltsgenehmigung* or *Aufenthaltserlaubnis*).

Tax
Double taxation agreement with UK.

Social security

Agreement with the UK under EC regulations (Ref: leaflet SA29). To take advantage of state health scheme you must register with the local Allgemeine Ortskrankenkasse (AOK) or Ersatzkasse which will issue you with a *Krankenschein* (entitlement document). You take this to any doctor or dentist participating in the scheme for free treatment. Some people supplement the state scheme with private insurance.

House purchase

House ownership is much less common than in the UK. Buyers usually go through estate agents (*Makler*), and the contract must be checked by a notary.

UK state pension

Payable at rate prevailing in the UK.

Reference

Living in Germany, J A S Abecasis-Philips (Robert Hale). *Living and Working in Germany* (Survival Guides).

GIBRALTAR

Population: 30,000   Area: 2.25 sq miles (6 sq km)
International dialling code: 00 350
A British enclave in the sun complete with bobbies and red post boxes which is currently being enlarged. Gibraltar is also an important financial centre and a good base for exploring Spain and Portugal.

Gibraltar representation in the UK

Tourist Office: 179 The Strand, London WC2R 1EH.
   Tel: (020) 7836 0777.

Social security

A reciprocal health service agreement is in operation. Further details are available from the Department of Labour and Social Security, 23 Mackintosh Square, Gibraltar. Tel: 00 350 78583.

Tax
There is no double taxation agreement with the UK.

Immigration
'Citizens of the UK may be granted at the Governor's discretion a permanent certificate of residence if they are of good standing and an asset to the community.' Further information is available from the Principal Immigration Officer, Treasury Building, Secretary's Lane, Gibraltar.

Property
Because of the restricted space property tends to be expensive and high rise. Conveyancing follows British practice and an offer should always include a 'subject to contract' let out clause.

GREECE

Population: 10 million   Area: 50,944 sq miles (131,944 sq km)
International dialling code: 00 30
Greece is about the same area as England, but 20% of the country is made up of islands. The latter may be fine as holiday destinations, but because many have restricted facilities, a villa on the mainland or one of the larger islands might prove a better choice for permanent residence unless you really want to get away from it all.

Greek representation in the UK
Embassy: 1A Holland Park, London W11 3TP. Tel: (020) 7727 8040.
Tourist Office: 4 Conduit Street, London W1R 8DL. Tel: (020) 7734 5997.

British representation in Greece
Embassy: 1 Ploutarchou Street, 10675 Athens. Tel: 00 30 1 723 6211.

Consulates: 2 Alexandras Avenue, 49100 Corfu. Tel: 00 30
   661 30055.
   16 Papa Alexandrou Street, 71202 Heraklion, Crete.
   Tel: 00 30 81 224 012 25.
   Martiou Street No 23, PO Box 47, 85100 Rhodes.
   Tel: 00 30 241 27247.
   8 Venizelou Street, Eleftheria Square, PO Box 10332,
   54110 Salonika. Tel: 00 30 31 278006.
   8 Akti P Ralli, Ermoupolis, 84100 Syros. Tel: 00 30 281
   222321.
   4 Iolou Street, 38221 Volos. Tel: 00 30 421 24642.

Immigration requirements

In accordance with EC rules you can stay in Greece for up to
three months and then apply to the Aliens Bureau in Athens
or the local police for a temporary residence permit. When
you have resided in Greece for two years you become elegible
for a permanent residence permit.

Health

You should submit your E121 form to IKA, the local office
of the Social Insurance Foundation (head office: 64 Piraeus
Street, 10436 Athens) and obtain a medical booklet and the
name of a doctor or dentist who works for the social
insurance scheme. For prescriptions you will be charged 20%
of the cost.

   Because of the long waits for treatment at clinics and
hospitals many people opt for private treatment, in which
case you must take out private medical insurance.

Tax

There is a double taxation agreement with the UK.

House purchase

This follows similar lines to Spain and Portugal. Once you
have agreed terms in principle with the vendor you or your
representative instructs the notary. The latter, who has to be
paid in advance by the purchaser, investigates the titles to the
property, prepares the contract and calculates any tax

payable. The contract has to be signed in the presence of the notary by you or your legal representative and then registered with the land registry office. In order to avoid slip ups it is highly advisable to engage the services of a lawyer to act on your behalf. Legal costs will add perhaps 15% to the cost of the house.

Reference
Buying a Home in Greece and Cyprus (Survival Books).
Living and Working in Greece, Peter Reynolds (How To Books).
Athens Daily Post, 57 Stadiou Street, Athens. Tel: 00 30 1 324 9504. Website: www.athensnews.dolnet.gr.

IRISH REPUBLIC

Population: 3.5 million   Area: 27,136 sq miles (70,283 sq km)
International dialling code: 00 353
The Emerald Isle is so close that you tend to overlook its potential as a place for retirement.

Irish representation in the UK
Embassy: 17 Grosvenor Place, London SW1X 7HR.
    Tel: (020) 7235 2171.
Tourist Board: 150 New Bond Street, London W1Y 0AQ.
    Tel: (020) 7493 3201.

British representation in Ireland
Embassy: 31 Merrion Road, Dublin 4. Tel: 00 353 1 695211.

Immigration restrictions
No restrictions for people born in an EU member state or who have at least one parent or grandparent born in Ireland.

Buying property
The following organisations will be able to recommend agents and solicitors:
    Irish Auctioneers' and Valuers' Institute, 38 Merrion

Square East, Dublin 2. Tel: 00 353 1 611794.
Incorporated Law Society of Ireland, Blackhall Place,
Dublin 7. Tel: 00 353 1 710711.

Major Irish newspapers which carry property advertising:
The Irish Press/Evening Press, Tara House. Dublin 2. Tel:
00 353 1 713333. 72 Fleet Street, London EC4. Tel: (020)
7353 4539.
Irish Independent/Evening Herald, 90 Middle Abbey Street,
Dublin 1. Tel: 00 353 1 731666. 292 Vauxhall Bridge
Road, London SW1. Tel: (020) 7828 4070.
Irish Times, 11 D'Olier Street, Dublin 2. Tel: 00 353 1
6792022. 76 Shoe Lane, London EC4 1LB. Tel: (020) 7353
8981.
Cork Examiner/Evening Echo, 95 Patrick Street, Cork.
Tel: 00 353 21 272722.

Imports
For full details regarding importation of goods under the
transfer of residence provisions consult the Revenue
Commissioners Notice No 153 obtainable from the Revenue
Commissioners, Division 1, Dublin Castle, Dublin 2.
Tel: 00 353 1 6792777.

Tax
There is a double taxation agreement. Rates are comparable
with the UK. If you are an artist or writer you may not need
to pay income tax at all.

Health provision
There are two eligibility categories for health services:

- *full eligibility* – eligibility for this category is means
  tested and those eligible are issued with a medical card
  which entitles you to free health treatment in most cases;
- *limited eligibility* – people in this category are not
  normally issued with a medical card; however EC
  pensioners may be entitled to one regardless of the
  amount of their pension.

For more information contact the Health Board of the locality where you are living.

Reference
Buying a Home in Ireland (Survival Guides).

ISLE OF MAN

Population: 65,000   Area: 221 sq miles (588 sq km)
A self-governing Crown dependency which does not suffer from overcrowding in the same way as the Channel Isles.

Useful address: Isle of Man Government, Government House, Bucks Road, Douglas, IOM. Tel: (01624) 26262.

The Isle of Man Government produces a *General Information Factfile* which includes addresses of estate agents, solicitors, banks and other facilities as well as a guide to property prices.

Immigration
There are no restrictions on UK citizens.

Tax
There is a double taxation agreement with the UK.

Social security
There is a reciprocal agreement with the UK. Health care is provided along similar lines to the NHS. For further details contact Department of Health & Social Security, Markwell House, Douglas, Isle of Man.

House purchase
No restrictions. Conveyancing follows similar lines to the UK, but because Manx property laws differ from those of the UK (being based on Norse law) it is advisable to engage the services of an advocate (solicitor).

ITALY

Population: 57 million   Area: 116,304 sq miles (301,225 sq km)
International telephone code: 00 39
Italy with its history, culture and climate has always attracted expatriates. Le Marche, Tuscany and Umbria are especially popular with the British. The lake areas in the north tend to be expensive, but there is a small British community by Lake Como. A knowledge of Italian is a must.

Italian representation in the UK

Embassy: 14 Three Kings Yard, Davies Street, London W1Y 2EH. Tel: (020) 7312 2200.
Consulate General: 38 Eaton Place, London SW1. Tel: (020) 7235 9371.
    6 Melville Crescent, Edinburgh EH3 7JA. Tel: (0131) 226 3631.
Consulate: 111 Piccadilly, Manchester M1 2HY. Tel: (0161) 236 9024.
Vice Consulate: 7–9 Greyfriars, Bedford MK40 1HJ. Tel: (01234) 56647.
Tourist Office: 1 Princes Street, London W1R 8AY. Tel: (020) 7408 1254.
Institute of Culture: 39 Belgrave Square, London SW1X 8NX. Tel: (020) 7235 1461.

British representation in Italy

Embassy: 80a Via Venti Settembre, 00187 Rome. Tel: 00 39 06 482 5441.
Consulates: 87 Via San Lucifero, 09100 Cagliari, Sardinia. Tel: 00 39 70 662755.
    2 Lungarno Corsini, 50123 Firenze. Tel: 00 39 055 284133.
    28 Via di Francia, 16149 Genoa. Tel: 00 39 010 605 3305.
    7 Via San Paolo, 20121 Milano. Tel: 00 39 02 723001.
    122 Via Francesco Crispi, 80122 Napoli. Tel: 00 39 081 663511.
    6 Via Dante Aligheri, 34122 Trieste. Tel: 00 39 040 347 8303.

1051 Accademia, 30123 Venezia. Tel: 00 39 041 522 7207.

House purchase

1. Document of intent. The *contratto preliminare di vendita* or *compromesso di vendita* is a legally binding contract to purchase the property on the terms laid down in the document.
2. Enquiries are made at the local land registry (*registro immobiliare*) to verify title, planning consent, outstanding charges on the property, etc. (This could also be done before stage 1.) You will be expected to pay a deposit – *caparra penitenziale* – which is non-refundable. Note that if you pay a *caparra penetenziale* you are legally obliged to go ahead with the purchase.
3. The formal conveyance – *scritura privata* or *atto di conpravendita* – is signed in the presence of a notary.
4. The notary registers the conveyance at the stamp duty office (*ufficio del registro*) and gives you a copy. You will be required to pay Land Registry fees, *imposta di registro*. It is advisable to engage the services of a lawyer and also a surveyor (*geometra*) before you sign the initial *compromesso*.

   Taxes and fees can typically add around 15% to the purchase price (eg land registry tax: 4–19% of declared value of property; notary's fees: 2–4%; estate agent's fees: 3–5%). VAT (10–20%) is payable on new property.

Immigration restrictions

None. EU nationals can live in Italy for an indefinite period. You must obtain a residence permit (*permesso di soggiorno*) from the police authorities (*questura*) in the area in which you intend to reside. You are also entitled to a certificate of residence from the municipality (*comune*) which will enable you to import personal effects duty-free if presented to the Italian customs.

Tax

Double taxation agreement with UK.

Social security

Agreement with the UK (Ref: leaflet SA29). To obtain treatment under the state health service you need to obtain a certificate of entitlement to the local *Unità Sanitaria Locale* (USL) office. This must be presented to any doctor or dentist participating in the scheme. Medical facilities tend to vary from place to place, and you may decide to take out private insurance to get speedier treatment.

UK state pension

Payable at rate prevailing in the UK.

Reference

Buying a Home in Italy (Survival Guides).
Living and Working in Italy (Survival Guides).
Living and Working in Italy, Victoria Pybus (Vacation Work).
Living and Working in Italy (How To Books).

MADEIRA

Population: 270,000   Area: 314 sq miles
International dialling code: 00 351 291
A group of islands in the Atlantic that are autonomous regions of Portugal.

British representation

Consulate: Avendia de Zarco 2, CP 417, 9000 Funchal. Tel:
00 351 291 21221.

See Portugal entry for further details.

MALTA & GOZO

Population: 375,000   Area: 122 sq miles (316 sq km)
International dialling code: 00 356
There is still quite a British atmosphere on these islands in the centre of the Mediterranean. English is widely spoken in addition to Maltese (which is closely related to Arabic) and

the cost of living remains relatively low. The government seems keen to attract wealthy British settlers!

Maltese representation in UK
High Commission: 36–38 Piccadilly, London W1V. Tel: (020) 7292 4800.

British representation in Malta
High Commission: 7 St Anne Street, Floriana, Malta.

Immigration
Three kinds of residence status:
- *Non-resident* – if you stay less than six months in Malta during a calendar year you have no tax liability.
- *Temporary resident* – you can live here indefinitely by renewing your visa periodically. You may need to show documentary evidence of your financial situation (eg bank statements) and will be subject to Maltese income tax if you reside here for more than six months in a calendar year.
- *Permanent resident* – to qualify for a permanent residence permit you need to have assets of £M150,000 or a minimum income of more than £M10,000 of which £M6,000 must be remitted to Malta.

House purchase
Non-Maltese citizens may purchase property in Malta or Gozo, but the purchase price must be in excess of £M30,000 for a flat and £M50,000 for a house. (In 2002 the Maltese pound was worth roughly £1.50 sterling. Housing is generally of a high standard.

House buying procedures proceed along the following lines.

1. A preliminary promise of sale agreement is signed which is valid for three months. A 10% deposit is lodged with an intermediary (estate agent, notary or legal adviser).
2. The notary undertakes searches and submits applications to government departments.

3. When searches prove satisfactory and permits are issued
the final contract is signed and the balance paid.

Duty, legal fees, etc amount to approximately 15%. The
vendor normally pays the estate agent's fees.

Tax
Double taxation agreement with UK.

Temporary residents only become liable for Maltese tax if
they stay more than six months. Permanent residents pay a
concessionary rate of tax of 15%.

Social security
Agreement with the UK (Ref: leaflet SA11 and SA28/30).
UK residents are entitled to receive state healthcare on the
same terms as Maltese nationals. For information about the
Maltese scheme contact: Director of Social Services, 310
Republic Street, Valetta, Malta.

UK state pension
Payable at rate prevailing in the UK.

Reference
Come Home to Malta (Ministry of Finance, Malta). Offers
up-to-date details on living conditions and bureaucratic
requirements.
The Times, Strickland House, 341 St Paul Street, PO Box
328, Valletta. Tel: 00 356 241464.

PORTUGAL

Population: 10.5 million   Area: 35,553 sq miles (92,082 sq
km)
International dialling code: 00 351
Like Spain, Portugal is no longer as cheap as it used to be.
There has been considerable development in the Algarve,
some of it by British developers, and people are retiring there
in increasing numbers. The eastern Algarve is still relatively

undeveloped. Madeira is also popular and there are sizeable British communities in Lisbon and Oporto.

Portuguese representation in the UK

Embassy: 11 Belgrave Square, London SW1X 8PP. Tel: (020) 7235 5331.

Consulate-General and consulates: Silver City House, 62 Brompton Road, London SW3 1BJ. Tel: (020) 7581 8722.

Alexandra Court, 93A Princess Street, Manchester M1 4HT. Tel: (0161) 834 1821.

25 Bernard Street, Edinburgh. Tel: (0131) 555 2080.

National Tourist Office: 22–25A Sackville Street, London W1X 1PE. Tel: (020) 7494 1441.

British representation in Portugal

Embassy: Rua S Domingos à Lapa 35–37, 1200 Lisbon. Tel: 00 351 21 396 1191.

Consulates: Avenida de Boavista 3072, 4100 Oporto. Tel: 00 351 22 68479.

Rua de Santa Isabel 21, 8500 Portimão, Algarve.

Tax

Double taxation agreement.

Social security

Agreement with the UK under EC regulations (Leaflet SA26). To obtain treatment on the state health service (CAIXA) you should visit the local Centro de Saúde. However, the refund payable is relatively small and it may be sensible to take out private medical insurance.

UK state pension

Payable at rate prevailing in the UK.

Immigration

European Union rules apply. Within three months of your arrival you must legalise your residence status with the Foreigners' Department (Servicos Estrangeiros).

House purchase

1. Developers (but not individual sellers) may ask you to sign an option on a property. You should check whether the deposit is refundable if you do not proceed with the purchase.
2. Searches at the Land Registry and municipal authority for title, charges, etc. Tax departments also have records of properties in their area.
3. Sign a promissory contract (*contrato promessa de compra e venda*). Notarial authentication of signatures may be needed. A non-refundable deposit is usually paid at this juncture.
4. Transfer of ownership. The title deed (*escritura publica de compra e venda*) is prepared and witnessed by a notary and should be checked carefully.
5. Registration of the title deed at the land registry. The notary will only do this if asked to.

It is always advisable to employ a legal adviser.

Note the following useful address: Association of Foreign Property Owners in Portugal, Apt 23, Alvor, 8800 Portimão.

Reference books

Blackstone Franks Guide to Living in Portugal, Bill Blevins and David Franks (Blackstone Franks).

Buying Property in Portugal, Rosemary de Rougemont (Banco Totta & Açores, 68 Cannon Street, London EC4N 6AQ. Tel: (020) 7236 1515).

A Guide to Buying Property in Portugal (Bennett & Co, Alderley Edge).

Living in Portugal, Susan Thackeray (Robert Hale).

Your Home in Portugal, Rosemary de Rougemont (Longman Money Guides).

Buying a Home in Portugal (Survival Guides).

Periodicals

Anglo-Portuguese News, APN Publicaçòes Lda, Apt 1133, Estoril P-2765. Tel: 00 351 21 344 3739.

Algarve News, Travelpress Europe Ltd, PO Box 13, Lagoa,

Algarve P-8400. Tel: 00 351 82 341100.

Portugal Post, Travelpress Europe Ltd, Rua 25 Abril, Lisboa
P-6200. Tel: 00 351 21 237 4961.

Algarve Property Advertiser, VIP, Urb Lagoa Sol, Lote 1-B,
8400 Lagoa, Portugal. Tel/Fax: 00 351 282 343088.

See also Azores and Madeira entries.

SPAIN

Population: 40 million   Area: 194,897 sq miles (504,782 sq
km)
International dialling code: 00 34
Spain (which includes the Balearic Islands and the Canary
Islands) has become a popular retirement location for
Northern Europeans, including tens of thousands of British
people. As a result there are a number of well established
expatriate communities, particularly on the Costa Blanca
(Alicante) and the Costa del Sol. The preferred locations
seem to be smaller coastal towns as well as small villages and
townships a few miles inland.

There has been a considerable amount of development
along the coast and consequently a wide range of
apartments and villas are on offer. Many of the latter are
on estates (urbanización) – some of them extensive with a
full range of facilities: shops, medical centre, management
office, etc. There is a shortage of old properties for
renovation.

Purpose-built retirement developments are a fairly new
phenomenon. They include the Colina Club at Calpe
(Alicante), Almond Court at Mutxamel (Alicante) by
Interspain, Jardines de Minea near Fuengirola built by Ove
Arkil and the extensive Ciudad Patricia at Benidorm. They
offer sheltered housing either in the form of linked villas or
flats and the first two either have or plan to have a nursing
home attached.

Spanish representation in UK

Embassy: 24 Belgrave Square, London SW1X 8QA.
Tel: (020) 7235 5555.
Consulates: 23 Manchester Square, London W1. Tel: (020)
7589 8989.
21 Rodney Street, Liverpool L1 9EF.
70 Spring Gardens, Manchester M2 2BQ. Tel: (0161) 236
1233.
Tourist Office: 57 St James's Street, London SW1A 1LD. Tel:
(020) 7499 0901.

British representation in Spain

Embassy: Calle de Fernando el Santo 16, 2800 Madrid.
Tel: 00 34 1 419 0200.
Consulates: Avda de la Fuerzas, Armadas 11, Algeciras.
Tel: 00 34 95 666 1600.
Plaza Calvo Sotelo 1/2–1, Apartado de Correos 564, 13001
Alicante. Tel: 00 34 6 521 6190.
Edificio Torre de Barcelona, Avenida Diagonal 477, 08036
Barcelona. Tel: 00 34 3 419 9044.
Alameda de Urquijo 2–8, Bilbao 8. Tel: 00 34 4 415 7600.
Edificio Duquesa, Duquesa de Parcent 4–1, Málaga.
Tel: 00 34 95 221 7571.
Paseo de Pereda 27, Santander. Tel: 00 34 94 222 0000.
Santian 4, Tarragon. Tel: 00 34 97 721 1246.
Plaza Compostela 23–6, Apartado 49, Vigo. Tel: 00 34 98
621 1450.

Tax

Double taxation agreement.

Social security

Agreement with the UK under EC regulations (Leaflet
SA29). In order to become eligible for treatment under the
Spanish health system you should register with the Dirección
Provincial del Instituto National de la Seguridad Social
(INSS) who will allocate you a GP.

UK state pension
Payable at rate prevailing in the UK.

House purchase
Spain has seen its share of property scandals in which people have handed over large sums of money to property developers who have promptly disappeared with the takings. You therefore need to exercise especial care doing business only with reputable firms (developers and/or licensed estate agents) and a lawyer (*abogado*) who will represent your interests and not those of the vendor.

1. If you are buying a new property you may be asked to sign an option on it. Check whether the deposit is refundable.
2. Title and planning searches at the Land Registry and municipal authorities. Your legal adviser should calculate liability to municipal tax (*plus valia*) and negotiate which party pays it. (This may take place after stage 3.)
3. Exchange of contracts. The *contrato privado* is a legally binding commitment to buy on the terms stated in the document, and a non-refundable deposit is normally payable.
4. Transfer of ownership. The *escritura publica de compravento* is prepared and witnessed by a notary.
5. The *escritura* has to be registered at the land registry. The notary will do this only if asked.

To understand the intricacies of house purchase Per Svensson's book *Buying and Selling Your Home in Spain* is indispensible.

Useful address
Institute of Foreign Property Owners (Instituto de Propietarios Extranjeros), Avenida Fermín Sanz Orrio 15-2-9, Apartado de Correos 418, 03590 Altea (Alicante). Tel: 00 34 96 584 2312. Fax: 00 34 96 584 1589.
An association with offices and local representatives throughout Spain which offers advice to expatriate property

owners (and prospective property owners). Its monthly bulletin provides up-to-date information on all matters affecting expatriates, including recent government legislation. It might turn out to be a shrewd move on your part to become a member before you actually take the plunge and buy a property.

Reference books

Blackstone Franks Guide to Living in Spain (Blackstone Franks).

Buying and Selling Your Home in Spain, Per Svensson (Longman).

Buying a Home in Spain (Survival Guides).

A Guide to Buying Property in Spain (Bennett & Co, Wilslow).

The Complete Guide to Buying a Property in Spain, A Foster (Property Search. Tel: (01223) 462244).

Living and Working in Spain, Robert Richards (How To Books).

So You Want to Live in Spain. Available from D F Rose, 27 Poets Chase, Aylesbury HP21 7LP. Tel: (01296) 336853.

Taxation in Spain, Andrew Hall (PKF, Guernsey).

Periodicals

Costa Blanca News, Edificio Astoria 2° n 3° Calle Dr Perez Lorca, Apdo 95, Benidorm E-03500 (Alicante). Tel: 00 34 96 585 5286.

The Entertainer, Era del Lugar, Mojacar, Almeira, E-04630. Tel: 00 34 951 478650.

Iberian Daily Sun, Ediciones Lemma SA, Zurbano 74, Madrid, E-28010.

See also Balearic Islands and Canary Islands entries.

SWITZERLAND

Population: 7.5 million   Area: 15,943 sq miles (41,293 sq km)

International dialling code: 00 41
Europe's most mountainous country enjoys a high standard
of living and is extremely well organised. Generally speaking,
it is an option for wealthier retirees.

Swiss representation in UK

Embassy: 16 Montagu Place, London W1H 2BQ. Tel: (020)
7616 6000. Visa information: 0906 833 1313.
Tourist Office: Swiss Centre, New Coventry Street, London
W1V 8EE. Tel: (020) 7734 1921.

UK representation in Switzerland

Embassy: Thunstrasse 50, 3005 Bern. Tel: 00 41 31 445021.
Consulates: 37–39 rue de Vermont, 1211 Geneva 20. Tel: 00
41 22 734 3800.
Dufourstrasse 55, 8008 Zurich. Tel: 00 41 1 261 1520.
Via Motta 19/Via Nassa 32, 6900 Lugano. Tel: 00 41 91
238606.

Immigration restrictions

Switzerland is not yet a member of the European Union, so
you should not assume that you have the right to settle there.
In order to retire there you must be able to prove you have
sufficient means to support yourself, be over 60 and own a
property in Switzerland. Initially you will have a B permit
which has to be renewed annually. After five years you
become eligible for a C permit.

House purchase

In recent years there have been quota restrictions on the
purchase of property by foreigners but these have been lifted.
However, some cantons are reluctant to let any foreigners
own property at all. Building is of a high standard, and as a
consequence property prices are high.

Tax

Double taxation agreement.

Social security
Agreement with the UK (Leaflet SA6). For information about Swiss medical benefits contact: Office Fédéral des Assurances Sociales, Effingerstrasse 33, 3000 Bern. Membership of a Swiss sickness assurance fund is compulsory in some cantons.

UK state pension
Payable at rate prevailing in the UK.

TURKEY

Population: 66 million   Area: 301,382 sq miles (780,576 sq km)
International dialling code: 00 90
Turkey, where Europe and Asia meet, has not become an expatriate retirement destination as yet, although the climate on the Aegean and Mediterranean coasts makes these areas ideal for this purpose. Property is cheap, the cost of living low and the people hospitable. There is a sizeable British community in bustling Istanbul, where winters are much harsher than on the coast. Off the tourist beat there can be a language problem.

Turkish representation in the UK
Embassy: 43 Belgrave Square, London SW1X 8PA. Tel: (020) 7393 0202.
Consular Section: Rutland Lodge, Rutland Gardens, London SW7 1BW. Tel: (020) 7589 0360.
Turkish Government Tourist Office: 1st floor, 170–173 Piccadilly, London W1V 9DD. Tel: (020) 7629 7771.

British representation in Turkey
Embassy: Şehit Ersan Caddesi 46A, Ankaya, Ankara.
British Consulate-General: Tepebaşi. Beyoglu, Istanbul.
British Vice-Consulate: Izmir.

Immigration

Application for a residence permit has to made to the
Turkish Foreign Office through the Embassy. Each case is
considered on its merits.

Tax

Double taxation agreement.

Property purchase

Foreigners are allowed to buy freehold property within towns
or municipal areas. Outside the municipal areas you can only
buy leasehold. It is sensible to engage a lawyer to negotiate
the price for you and also look after legal matters.

Social security

Agreement with the UK (Leaflet SA22). For information
about the Turkish scheme contact: Sosyal Sigortalar Kurumu
Genel, Mudurlugu, Ankara, Turkey.

UK state pension

Payable at the rate prevailing in the UK.

Language

Turkish, German and English are widely spoken.

Appendix B
Retirement Locations:
Rest of the World

COVERAGE

Australia
Canada
Caribbean:
Dependent
Territories
  Anguilla
  Bermuda
  British Virgin
    Islands
  Cayman Islands
  Montserrat
  Turks & Caicos
    Islands

Caribbean:
Independent
States
  Antigua &
    Barbuda
  Bahamas
  Barbados
  Dominica
  Grenada
  Jamaica
  St Lucia
  St Kitts & Nevis
  St Vincent & the
    Grenadines
  Trinidad &
    Tobago

Israel
New Zealand
South Africa
USA

AUSTRALIA

Population: 19 million   Area: 2,967,909 sq miles (7,686,800 sq km)
International dialling code: 00 61
A huge country with a vast range of scenery and climate which retains a certain British character. Tropical Queensland is a favourite retirement location for Australians. Perth in Western Australia enjoys a Mediterranean climate. Melbourne is sedate; Sydney very cosmopolitan. Land is cheap away from the main urban

areas, partly because there is so much of it around. More than 200,000 British pensioners reside in the country. The government offices of the different states in London are a useful source of information.

Case history
Mrs H cannot recommend Australia too highly as a retirement location: 'The Australians recognise that old people have skills and brainpower and they are well looked after. Life is quicker but people are more friendly. On first acquaintance, however, Aussies are inclined to be a bit bombastic and try to put you down. You have to stand up to them and then they are quick to accept you. Pensioners get one free rail pass a year to go anywhere they like.'

Australian representation in the UK
High Commission: Australia House, Strand, London WC2B
    4LA. Tel: (020) 7379 4334. Website: www.australia.org.uk
Tourist Office: 10 Putney Hill, London SW15. Tel: (0870) 556
    1434.

State Government Offices
New South Wales: Australian Centre, Strand, London WC2B
    4LA. Tel: (020) 7887 5871.
Queensland: 392–393 Strand, London WC2R 0LZ.
    Tel: (020) 7836 1333.
South Australia: Australia House, Strand, London WC2B 4LA.
    Tel: (020) 7836 3455.
Victoria: Victoria House, Melbourne Place, Strand, London
    WC2B 4LJ. Tel: (020) 7836 2656.
Western Australia: Australia Centre, Strand, London WC2B
    4LA. Tel: (020) 7240 2881.

UK representation in Australia
High Commission: Commonwealth Avenue, Canberra, ACT
    2600. Tel: 00 61 262 706666.

Immigration restrictions
There are no obstacles if you have children in Australia who will sponsor you, but self-supporting retirees need to

transfer a substantial amount of capital to support themselves and acquire accommodation for their use. A four year retirement visa is available, which is renewable provided you still meet the capital requirements (currently around £250,000).

Property purchase
This is more or less along UK lines. Generally speaking, property costs less in Australia.

Tax
Double taxation agreement.

UK state pension
Frozen at rate payable when you left UK or became entitled to it. The Australian government will eventually top it up – but only after you have resided in the country for ten years.

Useful address
British Australian Pensioners Association, PO Box 35, Christie's Beach, South Australia 5165. Website: www.britishpensions.org.au

Social security
Agreement with the UK (Ref: leaflet SA5). The Australian health service – Medicare – pays 85% of medical expenses amd you should obtain a Medicare card on arrival.

Reference
Living and Working in Australia, Laura Veltman (How To Books).
Living and Working in Australia (Survival Books).
Australian News, Outbound Newspapers, 1 Commercial Road, Eastbourne BN21 3XQ. Tel: (01323) 726040. Fax: (01323) 649249. Website: www.outboundpublishing.com
Australian Outlook, Consyl Publishing, 3 Buckhurst Road, Town Hall Square, Bexhill on Sea TN40 1QF. Tel: (01424) 223111. Fax: (01424) 224992.
New Zealand & Australia Migration News, Migration Bureau, 5

Manfred Road, London SW5 2RS. Tel: (020) 8874 2844.
The Financial and Migrant Information Service,
Commonwealth Bank of Australia, 85 Queen Victoria
Street, London EC4V 4HA (Tel: (020) 7710 3990) publishes
a cost of living and housing survey.

CANADA

Population: 30 million   Area: 3,849,646 sq miles (9,970,537
sq km)
International dialling code: 00 1
Canada covers a vast area, but retirees will make for one of
the areas where the winters are reasonably mild, such as
Vancouver or Toronto. The cost of living is higher than in
the UK, and heating is a particularly expensive item. If you
have a particular area in mind it would be sensible to
contact the office of the relevant Agent General for any
information you need.

Canadian representation in UK
High Commission: MacDonald House, 1 Grosvenor Square,
London W1X 0AB. Tel: (020) 7258 6600. Website:
www.canada.org.uk.
Immigration Department: 38 Grosvenor Street, London W1X
0AA. Tel: (020) 7409 2071.

Government offices
British Columbia: 1 Regent Street, SW1Y 4NS. Tel: (020) 7766
5900.
Manitoba: Website: www.gov.mb.ca.
New Brunswick: Website: www. gov.nb.ca.
Quebec: 59 Pall Mall, SW1Y 5HJ. Tel: (020) 7766 5900.
Ontario: Website: www.ontario-canada.com.
Saskatchewan: Website: www.gov.sk.can.

UK representation in Canada
British High Commission: Elgin Street, Ottawa, Ontario K1P
5K7. Tel: 00 1 613 237 1530.
Consulates: Suite 901, 1155 University Street, Montreal,

Quebec H3B 3A7. Tel: 00 1 514 866 5863.
Suite 1910, College Park, 777 Bay Street, Toronto, Ontario
M5G 2G2. Tel: 00 1 416 593 1290.
Suite 800, 111 Melville Street, Vancouver, British Columbia
V6E 3V6. Tel: 00 1 604 683 4421 111.
Aldershot Building, Winnipeg, Manitoba R3P 0E2.
Tel: 00 1 204 896 1380.

Immigration

There is a sponsorship scheme for close relatives of
Canadian citizens and residents. Otherwise you may have
problems in passing the points test for immigrants unless
you are able to make a substantial investment in the country
and have a private income. Applications have to be made to
embassies and high commissions abroad.

Tax

Double taxation agreement. There may be a state tax of
20% on property purchased by non-residents.

Social security

There is a limited agreement with the UK (Leaflet SA20).
Further information from Canadian High Commission.

UK state pension

This is frozen at the rate prevailing when you leave the UK.

Useful addresses

Canadian Alliance of British Pensioners, 605 Royal York Road,
    Suite 202, Toronto, Ontario, Canada M8Y 4G5. Website:
    www.britishpensions.com
The Golden Age Association, a multi-service organisation for
    over-sixties: 5700 Westbury Avenue, Montreal, Quebec
    H3W 3EB. Tel: 00 1 514 739 4731.

Reference

Canada News, Outbound Newspapers, 1 Commercial Road,
    Eastbourne BN21 3XQ. Tel: (01323) 726040. Website:
    www.outboundpublishing.com

The Caribbean

There are so many countries in the Caribbean that it is impossible to deal with them all within the scope of this book. I have therefore limited myself to Commonwealth countries where English is spoken rather than those which have come under Spanish, French or Dutch influence.

In order to make the task more manageable I have divided the islands into two groups: those which are still administered by Britain and those which are fully independent.

Reference

How to Live in the Caribbean, Sydney Hunt (Caribbean Publishing).

The Caribbean Handbook, Financial Times Caribbean, PO Box 1037, St John's, Antigua.

Caribbean Islands Handbook, Ben Box and Sarah Cameron, eds (Footprint Handbooks, Bath).

British Dependent Territories in the Caribbean

None of these islands or island groups is particularly large and their populations are correspondingly small. Generally speaking, a UK citizen can stay on one of these islands for up to six months and then may apply for permanent residence. Normally, you will need to provide evidence that you have sufficient income to support yourself. Unless otherwise stated, you should assume that your UK state pension will be frozen if you take up permanent residence. You will also be expected to pay for medical treatment, so medical insurance is vital. Where no official address in the UK is given you should contact the Immigration Department on the island direct or contact the Foreign and Commonwealth Office, King Charles Street, London SW1A 2AH. Tel: (020) 7270 1500. Website: www.fco.gov.uk.

ANGUILLA

Population: 11,000   Area: 35 sq miles
International dialling code: 00 1 264
A flat coralline island noted for the excellence of its beaches.

Addresses
Anguilla Tourist Office: 7 Westwood Road, London SW13
    0LA. Tel: (020) 8876 9025.
Chief Immigration Officer: Permanent Minister's Office, The
    Valley, Anguilla.

BERMUDA

Population 60,000   Area: 21 sq miles
International dialling code: 00 1 441
Not strictly speaking in the Caribbean but to the north of
it, Bermuda consists of about 100 small islands of which
only 20 are inhabited. The cost of living is high, property
(for outsiders) expensive and the climate sub-tropical.

Addresses
Bermuda Tourist Office: 46 Battersea High Street, London
    SW11. Tel: (020) 7771 7001.
Chief Immigration Officer: Immigration Department, Ministry
    of Home Affairs, Government Administration Building, 30
    Parliament Street, Hamilton HM12, Bermuda. Tel: 00 1 441
    295 5151. Fax: 00 1 441 295 4115.

Tax
There is no taxation apart from land tax.

Social security
There is an agreement with the UK (Leaflet SA23). For
information about the Bermudan social services contact:
Department of Social Insurance, PO Box 1537, Hamilton 5,
Bermuda. There is no state health service as such in
Bermuda.

UK state pension

Payable at the rate prevailing in the UK.

BRITISH VIRGIN ISLANDS

Population: 13,000   Area: 59 sq miles
International dialling code: 00 1 340
A group of 46 islands east of Puerto Rico of which just 11
are inhabited. Thanks to the Trade Winds the climate is
pleasant and healthy.

For details of residence contact: Chief Migration Officer,
    Government Offices, Road Town, Tortola, BVI. Tel: 00 1
    340 43701.

(NB: The US Virgin Islands – population 106,000; area 132
sq miles – belong to the United States. Representation in
the UK: 25 Bedford Square, London WC1B 3HG. Tel:
(020) 7637 8481.)

CAYMAN ISLANDS

Population: 20,000   Area: 100 sq miles
International dialling code: 00 1 345
The three islands – Grand Cayman, Cayman Brac and Little
Cayman, lie in the western Caribbean south of Cuba and
are an offshore tax haven and financial centre. Unlike many
other islands in the area they are fairly flat. The
Government Information Services publish a useful
introduction: *Living in the Cayman Islands.*

Goverment Office in UK

6 Arlington Street, London SW1A 1RE. Tel: (020) 7491 7772.

For further information on residence requirements contact:
    Chief Immigration Officer, PO Box 1098, Grand Cayman,
    Cayman Islands. Tel: 00 1 345 98344.

MONTSERRAT

Population: 12,000   Area: 38 sq miles
International dialling code: 00 1 664
This mountainous volcanic island discovered by Columbus in 1493 has hot springs and lies in the eastern Caribbean. It has become an important regional communications centre and manufactures electronic components.

Addresses

Montserrat Government Office: 30b Wimpole Street, London
    W1. Tel: (020) 7224 5226.
Chief Immigration Officer: Government HQ, Plymouth,
    Montserrat. Tel: 00 1 664 2444.

TURKS & CAICOS ISLANDS

Population: 14,000   Area: 166 sq miles
International dialling code: 00 1 649
These 30 islands (just eight of which are inhabited) lie to the north of the Dominican Republic and Haiti. The main island is Grand Turk, and the climate is regarded as excellent with low humidity.

For further information on settlement contact: Chief
    Immigration Officer, Immigration Department, South Base,
    Grand Turk, TCI. Tel: 00 1 649 2939.

Independent Countries in the Caribbean

On the whole these are larger and more populous than the British dependent territories, but in many of them British influence is still strong. It is worth noting that most do not have reciprocal social security arrangements with the UK and that your UK state pension is likely to be frozen if you take up permanent residence. You will also need to take out private medical insurance. Retirees would appear to be welcome in all of them, but you must have sufficient means to live there.

ANTIGUA AND BARBUDA (State of)

Population: 68,000   Area: 170 sq miles
International dialling code: 00 1 268
Part of the Leeward Islands in the eastern Caribbean with a drier climate than most of the Caribbean, Antigua in particular is a well developed retirement location with direct air services to Europe.

Antiguan representation in the UK
15 Thayer Street, London W1M 5LD. Tel: (020) 7486 7073.

British representation in Antigua
38 St Mary's Street, PO Box 483, St John's. Tel: 00 1 268 462 0008.

Tax
Double taxation agreement.

THE BAHAMAS (Commonwealth of)

Population: 300,000   Area: 5,380 sq miles
International dialling code: 00 1 242
The archipelago to the east of Florida consists of 700 islands, 30 of them inhabited. The island of San Salvador was Columbus' first encounter with the New World. Summers can be very humid. The cost of living is lower than in the UK and the country is a tax haven.

Bahaman representation in the UK
High Commission: 10 Chesterfield Street, London W1X 8AH. Tel: (020) 7408 4488.
Tourist Office: 23 Old Bond Street, London W1X 4PQ. Tel: (020) 7269 5238.

British representation in the Bahamas
High Commission: Ansbacher House, East Street, PO Box N7516, Nassau. Tel 00 1 242 325 7471.

For further information on residence contact: Director of
Immigration, PO Box 831, Nassau, Bahamas.

BARBADOS

Population: 270,000   Area: 166 sq miles
International dialling code: 00 1 246
The most easterly of the Caribbean islands is one of the
oldest democracies in the Commonwealth. Taxation is fairly
low – no capital gains tax or inheritance tax – but you have
to pay purchase tax on houses. There is an international
airport on the island.

Barbadan representation in the UK
High Commission: 1 Great Russell Street, London WC1B
    3NH. Tel: (020) 7631 4975.
Tourist Office: 263 Tottenham Court Road, London W1P 9AA.
    Tel: (020) 7636 9448.

British representation in Barbados
High Commission: Lower Collymore Rock, PO Box 676,
    Bridgetown. Tel: 00 1 246 436 6694.

Pension
British state pensions are paid at the rate prevailing in the
UK.

Tax
Double taxation agreement.

DOMINICA (Commonwealth of)

Population 75,000   Area: 290 sq miles
International dialling code: 00 1 767
The mountainous island of Dominica – not to be confused
with the much larger Dominican Republic – lies between the
French speaking islands of Guadeloupe and Martinique in
the Windward Group. It was a French colony until 1814,

and a French *patois* is still spoken there.

According to Sydney Hunt (author of *How to Live in the Caribbean*): 'Of all the islands in our beautiful Caribbean, Dominica stands unique as the one least troubled by the modern age...persons who may wish to retire here...can count on a peace and serenity that they have probably never encountered anywhere else.'

Dominican representation in the UK
High Commission: 1 Collingham Gardens, London SW5 OHW.
    Tel: (020) 7370 5194.
Tourist Office: address as above. Tel: (020) 7835 1937.

British representation
See Barbados entry.

GRENADA (State of)

Population: 96,000   Area: 133 sq miles
International dialling code: 00 1 473
Colonised by the French and ceded to Britain by the Treaty of Versailles in 1783 Grenada lies to the north of Trinidad. The island is mountainous and picturesque with a good climate, but has experienced political turbulence in recent years.

Grenadan representation in the UK
High Commission: 1 Collingham Gardens, London SW5 0HW.
    Tel: (020) 7373 7808.

British representation in Grenada
High Commission: 14 Church Street, St George's. Tel: 00 1 473 440 3222.

Tax
Double taxation agreement.

JAMAICA

Population: 2.5 million   Area: 4,411 sq miles
International dialling code: 00 1 876
The largest English-speaking country in the Caribbean lies
to the south of Cuba and has two international airports.

Jamaican representation in the UK
High Commission: 1–2 Prince Consort Road, London SE7 2BZ.
  Tel: (020) 7823 9911.

British representation in Jamaica
High Commission: PO Box 575, Trafalgar Road, Kingston 10.
  Tel: 00 1 876 926 9050.

Tax
Double taxation agreement.

Social security
Agreement with the UK (Leaflet SA27). For information
about Jamaican scheme contact: Ministry of Pensions and
Social Security, 14 National Heroes Circle, PO Box 10,
Kingston 5.

UK state pension
Paid at rate prevailing in the UK.

ST KITTS & NEVIS (Federation of)

Also known as St Christopher and Nevis
Population: 45,000   Area: 101 sq miles
International dialling code: 00 1 869
Two islands lying close to each other in the northern part of
the Leeward Islands in the eastern Caribbean with plenty of
sandy and coral beaches and a mountainous interior. The
hot tropical climate is tempered by the Trade Winds.

St Kitts representation in the UK
High Commission: 10 Kensington Court, London W8 5DL. Tel:

(020) 7937 9522.

British representation
High Commission, Antigua.

For further information on residence contact: Permanent
Secretary, Ministry of Foreign Affairs, Government
Headquarters, Basseterre, St Kitts & Nevis.

Tax
Double taxation agreement.

ST LUCIA

Population: 160,000   Area: 283 sq miles
International dialling code: 00 1 758
Situated to the south of Martinique in the eastern
Caribbean St Lucia is a mountainous island covered with
tropical vegetation. Britain and France vied for possession
of the island for a century and a half and there is still
French influence in the southern part of the island. The
island is served by international airlines.

St Lucia representation in the UK
High Commission: 10 Kensington Court, London W8 5DL. Tel:
(020) 7937 9522.
Tourist Office: 421a Finchley Road, London NW3.
Tel: (020) 7431 3675.

British representation in St Lucia
High Commission: NIS Waterfront Building, Castries.
Tel: 00 1 758 22484.

For further information on residence contact: Permanent
Secretary, Ministry of Foreign Affairs, Government
Building, Castries, St Lucia.

ST VINCENT & THE GRENADINES (State of)

Population: 120,000   Area: 133 sq miles
International dialling code: 00 1 784
A chain of 32 islands and islets to the north of Grenada and
Trinidad. The main ones – apart from St Vincent itself – are
Bequia, Mustique, Canouan, Mayreau, Pal and Union.
Some are privately owned.

St Vincent representation in the UK
High Commission: 10 Kensington Court, London W8 5DL. Tel:
    (020) 7937 2874.
Tourist Office: address as above. Tel: (020) 7937 6570.

British representation in St Vincent
High Commission: Granby Street, PO Box 132, Kingstown. Tel:
    St Vincent 00 1 784 71701.

For further information on residence contact: Permanent
    Secretary, Ministry of Foreign Affairs, Government
    Building, Kingstown, St Vincent & the Grenadines.

TRINIDAD & TOBAGO (Republic of)

Population: 1.3 million   Area: 1,980 sq miles
International dialling code: 00 1 868
The most southerly of the Caribbean islands lie just off the
Venezuelan coast. Trinidad – and particularly its capital,
Port of Spain, is a dynamic multi-racial place. Tobago to
the north is much quieter. The country has an international
airport.

Trinidad & Tobago representation in the UK
High Commission: 42 Belgrave Square, London SW1X 8NT.
    Tel: (020) 7245 9351.
    E-mail: trintogov@tthc.demon.co.uk.
Tourist Office: 20 Lower Regent Street, London SW1Y 4PH.
    Tel: (020) 7839 7155.

British representation in Trinidad & Tobago
High Commission: 19 St Clair Avenue, PO Box 778, Port of
    Spain. Tel: 00 1 868 625 28616.

Tax
Double taxation agreement.

Reference
Rough Guide to Trinidad and Tobago (Rough Guides).

ISRAEL

Population: 6 million   Area: 8,019 sq miles (20,770 sq km)
International dialling code: 00 972
Retirement to Israel will appeal to people who have a strong
emotional attachment to the country. However, given the
country's location and Middle Eastern politics it is by no
means the safest place to settle.

Israeli representation in the UK
Embassy: 2 Palace Green, London W8 4QB. Tel: (020) 7957
    9500. Website: www.israel-embassy.org.uk/london.
Israeli Government Tourist Office: 180 Oxford Street, London
    W1. Tel: (020) 7299 1111.

British representation in Israel
Embassy: 193 Hayarkon Street, Tel Aviv 63405.

Jews interested in retiring to Israel should contact the Aliyah
    Department, Balfour House, 741 High Road, North
    Finchley, London N12 0BQ. Tel: (020) 8343 9756.

Tax
Double taxation agreement.

Social security
Agreement with the UK (Leaflet SA14). For information
about Israeli scheme contact: Department of International
Conventions, National Insurance Institute, 13 Weizmann

Avenue, Jerusalem 91900.

UK state pension
Payable at rate prevailing in the UK.

NEW ZEALAND

Population: 4 million   Area: 102,344 sq miles
International dialling code: 00 64
New Zealand's climate is not dissimilar to that of the UK,
but the winters tend to be milder. By contrast, the country
is underpopulated, and three-quarters of the population
reside in the North Island. Like the UK the country has a
comprehensive health service paid for out of general
taxation.

New Zealand representation in the UK
High Commission: New Zealand House, Haymarket, London
SW1Y 4TQ. Tel: (020) 7930 8422. Immigration Service: Tel:
(020) 7973 0366.

British representation in New Zealand
High Commission: 44 Hill Street, PO Box 8612, Wellington 1.
Tel: 00 64 4 726049.

Immigration
Under present law there is no provision for granting
residence visas for people who wish to retire to New
Zealand unless they are eligible to join family members
already resident in the country. You will need to meet
health requirements and furnish evidence that you are a
person of good character.

House purchase
There are no restrictions on the purchase of property, and
the buying procedures are similar to those in England and
Wales.

Tax
Double taxation agreement with UK.

Social security
Agreement with the UK (Ref leaflet SA8). For information about New Zealand scheme contact: NZ High Commission. Immigrants are not normally eligible for social security until one year after arrival.

UK state pension
Frozen at rate payable when you left UK.

British Pensioners Association, PO Box 45274, Te Atatu Peninsula, Auckland 100. Tel: 0064 09834 8559. Website: www.britishpensionersnz.org.nz

Reference
Living and Working in New Zealand (How To Books).

New Zealand News UK, Commonwealth Publishing, New Zealand House, 80 Haymarket, London SW1Y 4TQ. (Tel: (020) 7930 6451). Publishes regular immigration supplements.

The New Zealand Immigration Book, Malcolm Consultants, 3rd Floor, 24–25 Bond Street, London W1Y 9HD. Tel: (020) 7267 3575.

New Zealand Outlook, Consyl Publishing, 3 Buckhurst Road, Town Hall Square, Bexhill on Sea TN40 1QF. Tel: (01424) 223111. Fax: (01424) 224992.

Destination New Zealand, Outbound Newspapers, 1 Commercial Road, Eastbourne BN21 3XQ. Tel: (01323) 726040. Fax: (01323) 649249. Website: www.outboundpublishing.com

New Zealand & Australia Migration News, Migration Bureau, Hyde Park House, 5 Manfred Road, London SW5 2RS. Tel: (020) 8874 2844.

The Financial and Migrant Information Service, Commonwealth Bank of Australia, 85 Queen Victoria Street, London EC4V 4HA (Tel: (020) 7710 3990) publishes a free information pack on New Zealand.

SOUTH AFRICA

Population: 46 million   Area: 471,445 sq miles (1,221,031 sq km)
International dialling code: 00 27
South Africa has an excellent climate and if the political future of the country looked more hopeful if would be an ideal place for retirement. Even so, some 30,000 British pensioners have made this their home. The two most popular retirement areas are Natal and the Garden Route in Cape Province. Property prices are low and so is the cost of living, which is partly attributable to the weakness of the rand.

South African representation in the UK
High commission: South Africa House, Trafalgar Square, London WC2N 5DP. Tel: (020) 7451 7299.

UK representation in South Africa
High Commission: 255 Hill Street, Arcadia, Pretoria 0002. Tel: 00 27 12 433121.
91 Parliament Street, Cape Town 8001. Tel: 00 27 21 461 7220.
Consulates: 16th Floor, Sanlam Centre, Cnr Jeppe and Von Wielligh Streets, Johannesburg 2000. Tel: 00 27 11 337 8940.
c/o Coopers & Lybrand, First National Bank Building, Union Street, East London 5201.
10th Floor, Fedlife House, 320 Smith Street, Durban 4001.

Immigration
Under present legislation to obtain a retiree permit you need

- to be sponsored by children or grandchildren already resident *or*
- to have sufficient funds to purchase a property and a recommended income of approximately £500 per person per month.

Applications are considered on individual merit and

arrangements usually take two months to finalise.

Useful address
British Retirement Pensioners Society (SA), PO Box 165,
Cramerview 2060, South Africa. Tel: 0027 11 792 8160.

House purchase
No restrictions. Conveyancing is simple and based on Dutch
law. The contract that you sign is binding and a non-
refundable 10% deposit is normally required. Estate agents
have to be qualified and licensed.

Tax
Double taxation agreement with the UK.

Reference
Living and Working in South Africa, Matthew Seal (How To
Books).
Living in South Africa and *This is South Africa* (Bureau for
Information Pretoria) obtainable from the South African
High Commission.
South Africa News, Outbound Newspapers Ltd, 1 Commercial
Road, Eastbourne, East Sussex BN21 3XQ. Tel: (01323)
726040. Website: www.outboundpublishing.com

USA

Population: 275 million   Area: 3,618,787 sq miles
(9,372,614 sq km)
International dialling code: 00 1
The United States is a large country but the most popular
retirement areas tend to be in the south and west, notably
Southern California, Arizona, Nevada, New Mexico and
Florida because of the mild winters. Florida has become a
particular favourite with the British of whom there are over
100,000 resident in this state – enough to support their own
expatriate newspaper *The Florida Brit*.

United States representation in the UK

Embassy: 24 Grosvenor Square, London W1A 2JB. Tel: (020)
7499 9000. Website: www.usembassy.org.uk.

Visa Branch: 5 Upper Grosvenor Street, London W1A 2JB.
Tel: (09061) 500590.

Consulate: Queen's House, Queen Street, Belfast BT1 6EQ. Tel:
(02890) 328239.
3 Regent Terrace, Edinburgh EH7 5BW. Tel: (01131) 557
6023.

US Information Service: 55/56 Upper Brook Street, London
W1A 2LH. Tel: (020) 7499 9000 ext 2643.

UK representation in the US

Embassy: 3100 Massachussetts Ave NW, Washington, DC
20009. Tel: 00 1 202 462 1340.

Consulates and Consulates-General: California: Suite 312, 3701
Wilshire Boulevard, Los Angeles, CA 9000. Tel: 00 1 213
385 7381.
1 Sansome Street, Suite 850, San Francisco, CA 94101. Tel:
00 1 415 981 3030.
Florida: Brickell Bay Office Tower, Suite 2110, 1001 S
Bayshore Drive, Miami, FL 33131. Tel: 00 1 305 374 1522.
Georgia: Suite 2700, Marquis One Tower, 245 Peach Tree
Centre Avenue, Atlanta, GA 30303.
Illinois: 400 North Michigan Avenue, Chicago, IL 60611.
Tel: 00 1 312 346 0810.
Massachusetts: 600 Atlantic Ave, Federal Reserve Plaza,
25th Floor, Boston, MA 02210. Tel: 00 1 617 437 7160.
New York: 845 Third Avenue, New York, NY 10022. Tel:
00 1 212 593 2258.
Texas: 1000 Louisiana Street, Suite 1900, Houston, TX
77002. Tel: 00 1 713 659 6270.
2911 Turtle Creek Blvd, Suite 940, Dallas, TX 75219. Tel:
00 1 214 637 3600.
Washington State: 999 3rd Ave, Suite 820, Seattle, WA
98104. Tel: 00 1 206 622 9255.

Immigration restrictions

As mentioned elsewhere in the book, it is difficult to acquire
permanent residence status in the United States unless you

are the spouse or child of an American citizen or the parents of a US citizen aged 21 or over. Other relations may be able to sponsor you, but expect a long wait.

If you are planning to make a sizeable investment – say $½ million plus – you may be able to achieve permanent residence in your own right. If you have not yet retired, buying a business or setting up on your own account may enable you to obtain a temporary visa (such as an L-1 or E-2 visa) and you will be able to petition for permanent residence status at a later date.

In all cases it is essential to take appropriate advice from an immigration lawyer or consultant. Appendix C has a list of UK-based ones or you could also contact: American Immigration Lawyers Association, 1400 I Street NW, Suite 1200, Washington DC 20005. Website: www.aila.org.

Even if you are unsuccessful, this need not mean the end to your dreams of living in the United States for extended periods. One option is to spend part of the year in the US and the rest in Europe, and rent out your property to holidaymakers when you are not in residence. EU citizens no longer require a visa for visits of up to three months. For stays up to six months a B-2 visa is required.

House purchase

If you can track it down, the Philpotts' book on house purchase in Florida is excellent reading and includes a guide to house purchase produced by the US Department of Housing which is relevant to other parts of the United States as well.

The Philpotts learned about house purchase the hard way – by making mistakes and losing money. As a result of their experiences they offer three important tips:

- 'Don't hand over any money unless it goes into an escrow account held by a licensed real estate broker...'
- 'Read everything carefully, never sign anything under pressure, and don't rush your decision.'
- Seek expert help from a... licensed real estate broker.'

By using a licensed broker to oversee every stage of the house purchase you are protected from loss as a result of the broker's actions. Some brokers also offer separate management, letting and maintenance services, and are thus able to look after your house when you are away. You should reserve the right to pick your own attorney (legal adviser).

Tax
Double taxation agreement with UK. You will also be subject to local taxes which may include the taxation of rental income.

Social security
There is a social security agreement with the US, but it does not include healthcare. Do not count on receiving Medicare benefits as a pensioner, but take out private medical insurance.

Reference
Buying a Home in Florida (Survival Guides).
Florida: The AIM Home Buyer's Guide, Don and Pam Philpott (Mediawise).
Getting a Job in America, Roger Jones (How To Books).
Getting into America, Henry Liebman (How To Books).
Living and Working in America, Steve Mills (How To Books).
Going USA, Outbound Newspapers, 1 Commercial Road, Eastbourne BN21 3XO. Tel: (01323) 726040. Website: outboundpublishing.com

Appendix C
Directory of Useful Addresses

COVERAGE

Associations and services
Education
Emigration advisers
Employment opportunities
Estate agents
Finance
Government departments (UK)
Holidays

Insurance
Language
Learning
Legal services
Property
Developers
Removals

ASSOCIATIONS AND SERVICES

Age Concern, Adastral House, 1268 London Road, London
SW16 4ER. Tel: (020) 8765 7200.
Website: www.ageconcern.org.uk.

Airpets Oceanic, Willowslea Farm Kennels, Spout Lane
North, Stanwell Moor, Staines, Middlesex TW19 6BW.
Tel: (01753) 685571. Pet travel agent.

Animal Angels, 8 Grand Parade, Station Road, Hook, Hants
RG27 9HT. Tel: (01256) 764141.
Website: www.animalangels.co.uk. Pet minding service.

Animal Aunts, Smugglers' Cottage, Rogate, Petersfield, Hants
GU31 5DA. Tel: (01730) 821529.
Website: www.animalaunts.co.uk. Pet minding service.

Association of Retired People, Greencoat House, Francis
Street, London SW1P 1DZ. Tel: (020) 7895 8880.

BBC World Service, PO Box 76, Bush House, Strand, London
WC2B 4PH. Tel: (020) 7240 3456.

Website: www.bbc.co.uk/worldservice.

Blair Consular Services Ltd, 31 Palace Street, London SW1. Tel: (020) 7630 5952. Visas.

British Australian Pensioners Association, PO Box 35, Christie's Beach, South Australia 5165.

British Retirement Pensioners Society (SA), PO Box 165, Cramerview 2060, South Africa. Tel: 0027 11 792 8160.

Canadian Alliance of British Pensioners, 605 Royal York Road, Suite 202, Toronto, Ontario, Canada M8Y 4G5.

Centre for International Briefing, Farnham Castle, Surrey GU9 0AG. Tel: (01252) 720416. Fax: (01252) 719277. Website: www.cibfarnham.com. E-mail: cibfarnham@dial.pipex.com. Country briefings.

Church of England Board for Social Responsibility (Overseas Resettlement Secretary), Church House, Dean's Yard SW1P 3NX. Tel: (020) 7898 1000. Contacts abroad.

Church of Scotland Overseas Council, 121 George Street, Edinburgh. Tel: (0131) 225 5722.

Golden Arrow Shippers, Horsford Kennels, Lydbury North, Shropshire SY 8AY. Tel: (01588) 680240. Fax: (01588) 680414. Pet transportation service.

The Good Book Guide, 24 Seward Street, London EC1V 3PS. Tel: (020) 7490 0900. Mail order book service.

Grace Consulting, Orchard House, Albury, Guildford GU5 9AG. Tel: (01483) 203666.

Help the Aged, St James's Walk, London EC1R 0BE. Tel: (020) 7253 0253.

Homesitters Ltd, Buckland Wharf, Aylesbury, Bucks HP22 5LQ. Tel: (01279) 777049. Website: www.homesitters.co.uk.

Housewatch, Little London, Berden, Bishops Stortford, Herts CM23 1BE. Tel: (01279) 777412.

Intercontinental Church Society, 1A Athena Drive, Tachbrook Park, Warwick CV34 6NL. Tel: (01926) 430347. Websites: www.ics-uk.org and www.churchesabroad.org.

Manor Car Storage, PO Box 28, Clavering, Saffron Walden, Essex CB11 4RA. Tel: (01799) 550021.

Methodist Church Overseas Division, 25 Marylebone Road, London NW1 5JR. Tel: (020) 7935 4521.

Par Air Services, Warren Way, Stanway, Colchester, Essex

CO3 5LN. Tel: (01206) 330332. Fax: (01206) 331277. Pet transport.

RADAR, 12 City Forum, 250 City Road, London EC1V 8AF. Tel: (020) 7250 3222. Website: www.radar.org.uk.

Stanfords, 12–14 Long Acre, London WC2E 9LP. Tel: (020) 7836 1321. Fax: (020) 7836 0189. Map and travel bookshop.

Universal Aunts, PO Box 304, London SW4 0NN. Tel: (020) 7738 8937. Personal services agency.

Women's Corona Society (Corona Worldwide), South Bank House, Black Prince Road, London SE1 7SJ. Tel: (020) 7793 4020. Website: www.commercepark.co.uk/coronaww/ Briefings and country reports.

Worldwide Animal Travel, 43 London Road, Brentwood, Essex CM14 4NN. Tel and Fax: (01277) 231611.

EDUCATION

ECIS (European Council for International Schools), 21 Lavant Street, Petersfield, Hants GU32 3EW. Tel: (01730) 268244. Publishes a directory of international schools.

Gabbitas Educational Consultants, Carrington House, 126–130 Regent Street, London W1R 6EE. Tel: (020) 7734 0161. Fax: (020) 7437 1764. Education advisers.

ISIS Independent Schools Information Service, 35 Grosvenor Gardens, London SW1W 0BS. Tel: (020) 7798 1500.

Mercers College, 14 Baldock Street, Ware, Herts SG12 9BU. Tel: (01920) 465926. Correspondence courses for young people.

Open University, PO Box 71, Walton Hall, Milton Keynes MK7 6AA. Tel: (0870) 333 0087. Website: www.open.ac.uk.

SFIA (School Fees Insurance Agency) Educational Trust Ltd, SFIA House, 15 Forlease Road, Maidenhead, Berks SL6 1JA. Tel: (01628) 34291. Publishers of *The Parent's Guide to Independent Schools*.

WES Home School, Blagrave House, 17 Blagrave Street, Reading, Berks RG1 1QA. Tel: (0118) 958 9993. Fax: (0118) 958 9994. Website: www.weshome.demon.co.uk.

E-mail: office@weshome.demon.co.uk.

EMIGRATION ADVISERS

Aaronson & Co, 308 Earls Court Road, London SW5 9BA. Tel: (020) 7373 9516. Fax: (020) 7835 1014. **USA**.

Ambler Collins, Eden House, 59 Fulham High Street, London SW6 3JJ. Tel: (020) 371 0213. Website: www.amblercollins.com. **Australia, Canada, New Zealand**.

Concept Australia, 3 Berryfield Close, Bromley, Kent BR1 2WF. Tel: (020) 8467 8521. Website: www.conceptaustralia.co.uk. **Australia**.

The Emigration Group, 7 Heritage Court, Lower Bridge Street, Chester CH1 1RD. Tel: (01244) 321414. Website: www. emigration.uk.com. **Australia, Canada, New Zealand**.

Frederick De Pasquale, Visa Services Inc, Devlin House, 36 St George Street, Mayfair, London W1R 9FA. Tel: (020) 7529 1423. Fax: (020) 7529 1402. Website: www.immigrationvisas.com. **USA**.

Gary M Ferman Law Office, 27 Bruton Street, London W1J 6QN. Tel: (020) 7499 5702. Fax: (020) 7236 2533. **USA**.

Four Corners Emigration, Freepost NWW 5817A, Cheadle SK8 1YG. Tel: (0845) 841 9453.
Website: www.4-corners.com. **Australia, Canada, New Zealand, USA**.

Global Visas, 181 Oxford Street, London W1D 2JT. Tel: (020) 7317 9497. Website: www.globalvisas.com.

Richard S Goldstein, 96A Mount Street, Mayfair, London W1X. Tel: (020) 7499 8200. Fax: (020) 7499 8300. **USA**.

Hemsley & Associates, 24A Bristol Gardens, London W9 2JQ. Tel: (020) 7266 4947. **New Zealand**.

Diane B Hinch, 24 Grosvenor Street, London W1X 9FB. Tel: (020) 7917 9680. Fax: (020) 7917 6002. **USA**.

Jaffe & Co, America House, 40 Hendon Lane, London N3 1TT. Tel: (020) 8371 0656. Fax: (020) 8371 9677. **USA**.

LaVigne, Coton & Associates, 150 Minories, London EC3N 1LS. Tel: (020) 7264 2110. Fax: (020) 7264 2107. **USA**.

Joel Z Robinson, 4 Helmet Row, London EC1V 3QV.

Tel: (020) 7253 2404. Fax: (020) 7253 0760. **USA**.

Migration Bureau, Hyde Park House, 5 Manfred Road, Putney, London SW15 2RS. Tel: (020) 8874 2844. **Canada, Australia, New Zealand**.

Vijay Sharma Solicitors, 142 Buckingham Palace Road, London SW1W 9TR. Tel: (020) 7730 7322. **Canada**.

Stan Steinger, 96 Kensington High Street, London W8 4SG. Mobile tel: (07956) 222572. **USA**.

David Turner, 12 Queen Anne Street, London W1M 0AU. Tel: (020) 7437 7076. Fax: (020) 7437 7079. **USA**.

Workpermit.com, 11 Bolt Court, Fleet Street, London EC4A 3DQ. Tel: (020) 7842 0800. Fax: (020) 7495 3991. Website: www.workpermit.com. **Australia, Canada, USA, etc**.

US Visa Consultants, 52 Maddox Street, London W1R 9PA. Tel: (020) 7317 6709. Fax: (020) 7317 6712. **USA**.

EMPLOYMENT OPPORTUNITIES

British Executive Service Overseas, 164 Vauxhall Bridge Road, London SW1V 2RB. Tel: (020) 7630 0644. Website: www.beso.org.

Department for International Development, Abercrombie House, Eaglesham Road, East Kilbride, Glasgow G75 8EA. Tel: (0845) 300 4100. Website: www.dfid.gov.uk.

i to i International Projects Ltd, 1 Cottage Road, Headingley, Leeds LS6 4DD. Tel: (0870) 333 2332. Fax: (0113) 274 6923 or (0870) 052 5760. Website: www.i-to-i.com.

Teaching & Projects Abroad Ltd, Gerrard House, Rustington, West Sussex BN16 1AW. Tel (01903) 859911. Fax: (01903) 785779. Website: www.teaching-abroad.co.uk.

VSO, 317 Putney Bridge Road, London SW15 2PN. Tel: (020) 8780 1331. Website: www.vso.org.uk.

ESTATE AGENTS (UK)

This is a select list of agencies which specialise in property abroad indicating the areas they deal with.

The acronym FOPDAC indicates that the firm is a

member of the Federation of Overseas Property Developers, Agents and Consultants, 3rd Floor, 95 Aldwych, London WC2B 4JF. Tel: (020) 8941 5588. Fax: (020) 8941 0202. Website: www.fopdac.com.

The acronym NAEA indicates that the firm is a member of the National Association of Estate Agents, Arbon House, 21 Jury Street, Warwick CV34 4EH. Tel: (01926) 496800. Fax: (01926) 400953. Website: www.naea.co.uk.

A House in France Ltd, 11 Mountview, London NW7 3HT. Tel: (020) 8959 5182. Fax: (020) 8906 8749. **France**.

Alexander Stephens Ltd, 213 Witan Gate East, Milton Keynes MK9 2HP. Tel: (01908) 607787. Fax: (01908) 393470. Website: www.alexanderstephens.co.uk. (NAEA) **Italy, Spain (including Balearics and Canary Islands), Portugal, USA: Florida.**

Alliance, 1 Hawthorn Road, Wallington, Surrey SM6 0SX. Tel: (020) 8669 6576. Fax: (020) 8669 5980. Website: www.firstforfrance.com. **France**.

Alpine Apartments Agency, Hinton Manor, Eardisland, Leominster, Herefordshire HR6 3BG. Tel: (01533) 388234. Fax: (01544) 388900. E-mail: zigi@aaa.kc3ltd.co.uk. (FOPDAC) **French Alps**.

Andrew Morris & Co, 1 Bridge Street, Hereford HR4 9DF. Tel: (01432) 266775. Fax: (01432) 344944. (NAEA) **Spain, France**.

Anglo Continental Properties, 55 Coten End, Warwick CV34 4NU. Tel: (0800) 085 2689. Website: www.anglocontinental.co.uk. Spain: **Costa Blanca**.

Atkins, 272 Wallisdown Road, Bournemouth BH10 4HZ. Tel: (01202) 548844. Fax: (01202) 548848. (NAEA) **USA: Florida**.

Atlas International, Atlas House, Station Road, Dorking, Surrey RG4 1EB. Tel: (01306) 879899. Fax: (01306) 877441. Website: www.atlas-international.com. **Spain**: **Costa Blanca**.

Authentic France, 27 Gresham Road, London E6 6DS. Tel/ Fax: (020) 8471 8600. **France**.

Beaches International Property Ltd, 3/4 Hagley Mews, Hagley

Hall, Hagley, W Midlands DY9 9LQ. Tel: (01562) 885181. Fax: (01562) 886724. E-mail: enquiries@beachesint. freeserve.co.uk. (FOPDAC) **France, Spain**.

Bishop & Co, Cathedral Quarters, 2–3 Queen Street, Derby DE1 3DL. Tel: (01332) 747474. Fax: (01332) 741184. Website: www.propertychoice.co.uk. **France**.

Blue Sky Homes, Ansteads Farm, Stancombe, Stroud GL6 7NG. Tel: (0845) 702 3908. Website: www.blueskyhomes.co.uk. **Spain: Costa Blanca**.

Brian French & Associates, The Nook, Sowerby Street, Sowerby Bridge, West Yorkshire HX6 3AJ. Tel: (0870) 730 1910. Fax: (0870) 730 1911. Website: www.brianfrench.com. (FOPDAC) **Italy, France (SW)**.

Bullock & Lees, 4 Wick Lane, Christchurch, Dorset BH23 1HX. Tel: (01202) 485187. Fax: (01202) 473671. (NAEA) **USA: Florida**.

Casa del Sol, 51 High Street, Emsworth, Hants PO10 7AN. Tel: (01243) 379797. Website: www.casadelsol.co.uk. **Spain: Mallorca, Menorca**.

Casa Travella, 65 Birchwood Road, Wilmington, Kent DA2 7HF. Tel: (01322) 60988. Fax: (01322) 667206. Website: casatravella.com. (FOPDAC) **Italy, including Liguirna Riviera, Tuscany, Rome**.

Cerro Novo, The Manor House, Evington, Westbury, Wilts BA13 4QW. Tel: (01380) 831411. Fax: (01380) 831455. Website: www.cerronovo.com. (NAEA) **Portugal: Algarve**.

Chalcross, 18 Market Place, Chalfont St Peter, Bucks SL9 9EA. Tel: (01753) 886335. Fax: (01753) 886336. Also at Gerrards Cross. (NAEA) **France**.

Christopher Morris, 5 Claremont Hill, Shrewsbury SY1 1RD. Tel: (01743) 241615. Fax: (01743) 352688. Website: www.christophermorris.net. (FOPDAC and NAEA) **Spain, including Costa del Sol, Costa Blanca, Costa Orihuela**.

Churchills, 10 High Street, Mexborough, South Yorkshire S64 9AS. Tel: (01709) 582880. Fax: (01709) 570604. Website: www.churchills-uk.com. (NAEA) **Spain, Italy**.

Connell International Homes, 82 High Street, Winchester S023 9AD. Tel: (01962) 842955. **France, Spain, USA: Florida**.

Courciers, 4–8 Station Road, South Norwood, London SE25 5AJ. Tel: (020) 8853 6333. Fax: (020) 8653 6057. (NAEA) **Spain, USA: Florida**.

Crete Property Consultants, 78 Gascony Avenue, London NW6 4NE. Tel: (020) 7328 1829. Fax: (020) 7328. 8209. Website: www.creteproperty.co.uk. (FOPDAC) **Greece, including Greek islands and Crete**.

Currie French Properties, 2 Fulbrooke Road, Cambridge CB3 9EE. Tel: (01223) 576084. Fax: (01223) 570332. E-mail: info@cfps.demon.co.uk. (FOPDAC) **France**.

David Headland Associates, 67 Wellingborough Road, Rushden, Northants NN10 9YG. Tel: (01933) 353333. Fax: (01933) 315191. Website: www.headlands.co.uk. (FOPDAC) **Portugal, Spain: Costa del Azahar**.

David Philips Overseas, 12 Crouch Hill, Stroud Green, London N4 4AU. Tel: (020) 7686 7676. Fax: (020) 7686 7566. Website: www.davidphilips.co.uk. **Spain**.

David Scott International, Deerhurst House, Epping Road, Roydon, Harlow, Essex CM19 5DA. Tel: (01279) 792162. Fax: (01279) 792318. Website: www.nerjaproperties.co.uk. (FOPDAC) **Spain: Nerja, Costa del Sol**.

Denholm, 197 Kensington, Kensington, Liverpool L7 2RF. Tel: (0151) 260 9411. Fax: (0151) 264 8975. (NAEA) **USA: Florida**.

Derek Light, 3 Avenue Parade, The Avenue, Sunbury on Thames, Middlesex. TW16 5HS. Tel: (01932) 785262. Fax: (01932) 780035. Offices also in Twickenham and Hounslow. (NAEA) **Spain**.

DLR Properties Overseas, 5 Manor Parade, Brightlingsea, Colchester, Essex CO7 0UD. Tel: (01206) 303049. Fax: (01206) 306090. Website: www.dlr-properties.co.uk. (FOPDAC) **Spain: Costa Blanca**.

DM Properties, 18 Golden Grove, Treboeth, Swansea SA5 9DG. Tel/Fax: (01792) 799990. (FOPDAC) **Spain, including Costa Blanca and Costa del Sol**.

Eden Villas, Springfield, 33 Tranent Grove, Dundee DD4 0XP. Tel/Fax: (01382) 505101. Mobile: 0771 254 2443. Website: www.edenvillas.co.uk. (FOPDAC) **Spain: Costa Blanca, Costa del Sol, Costa del Azahar; Canary Islands:**

Tenerife.

Edwards, 2 High Street, Lanark ML11 7EX. Tel: (01555) 661439. Fax: (01555) 661096. (NAEA) **France, Italy, Portugal, Spain, USA: Florida**.

Ellington International, 259 London Road, Portsmouth PO2 9HA. Tel: (02392) 639638. Fax: (02392) 639039. **Andorra, Spain, USA: Florida**.

Eugenie Smith International, Canada House Business Centre, 1 Carrick Way, New Milton, Hants BH25 6UD. Tel: (01425) 619132. Fax: (01268) 685273. Website: www.eugeniesmith.com. (FOPDAC) **Spain, Barbados, Caribbean, Florida**.

Euro Horizon, 7–15 Pink Lane, Newcastle upon Tyne NE1 5DW. Tel/Fax: (0191) 230 5553. (FOPDAC) **Spain: Costa del Azahar**.

European Villa Solutions, 618 Newmarket Road, Cambridge CB5 8LP. Tel: (01223) 514241. Fax: (01223) 562713. Website: www.europeanvs.com. (FOPDAC) **Spain (including Coasta Blanca, Costa del Sol, Andalucia, Balearics), Portugal (Algarve)**.

Exclusively Florida, 7 Chasewood Corner, Bussage, Stroud, Glos GL6 8JS. Tel: (01453) 886905. Fax: (01453) 887820. Website: www.exclusivelyflorida.co.uk. **USA: Florida**.

F I Grey & Son UK, St Ethelbert House, Rylands Street, Hereford HR4 0LA. Tel: (01432) 265599. Fax: (01432) 845640. Website: www.worldofflorida.co.uk. (FOPDAC) **USA: Florida**.

FIDALSA, 69 Astbury Road, London SE15 2NP. Tel: (020) 7635 1502. Website: www.fidalsa.com. **Spain: Costa Blanca**.

Fiesta Villas Direct, 51 Ocean Drive, Ferring, East Sussex BN12 5QP. Tel: (08000) 180309. Fax: (01903) 700413. Website: www.fiestavillas.com. (FOPDAC) **Spain: Costa Blanca**.

Florida International, Ashmead, 5 Glebe Road, Staines, Middlesex TW18 1BX. Tel: (01734) 451851. Fax: (01734) 452055. Website: www.floridahomes.co.uk. (FOPDAC) **USA: Florida; Bahamas**.

Florida Keys International Services, Unit 1, Meadowcroft, Tusmore, Bicester OX6 9SL. Tel: (01809) 345662. Fax:

(01869) 345046. Website: www.villas.glo.cc. **USA: Florida**.

Florida Property & Business Services Inc, Box 41, Chichester, West Sussex PO20 6ND. Tel/Fax: (01243) 536026. **USA: Florida**.

Florida Villas Sales & Rentals Ltd, 21a Hursley Road, Chandlers Ford, Eastleigh, Hants SO53 2FS. Tel: (02380) 266222. Fax: (07799) 528296. Website: www.floridavillassales.co.uk. (FOPDAC) **USA: Florida**.

Foremost Villas, 78 Hinton Wood Avenue, Highcliffe, Christchurch, Dorset BH23 5AJ. Tel/Fax: (01425) 275909. (FOPDAC) **Spain: Costa Blanca**.

Galerie International, 24 Wellington Road, Enfield, Middlesex EN1 2E. Tel: (020) 8367 0050. Fax: (020) 8367 3921. (FOPDAC) **Spain: Costa Blanca, Costa del Sol**.

Goffs, 208 Crookes, Sheffield S10 1TG. Tel: (0114) 266 7000. Fax: (0114) 266 6026. (NAEA) **Portugal, Spain**.

Greenbox International Ltd, TTMA House, Norham Road, North Shields, Tyne & Wear NE29 7UJ. Tel: (0191) 296 3838. Fax: (0191) 296 4848. Website: www.greenbox.co.uk. (FOPDAC) **Spain, Portugal**.

Halcyon Properties, 3 Dukes Close, Seaford, East Sussex BN25 2TU. Tel: (01323) 891639. Fax: (01323) 892954. Website: www.halcyon-properties.co.uk. (FOPDAC) **Greece, Cyprus**.

Harman Estates, 19 Elstree Gardens, Ilford, Essex IG1 2QQ. Tel/Fax: (020) 8553 2846. **Spain, USA: Florida**.

Hartman Homes Group, 10 The Plateau, Warfield Park, Bracknell, Berks RG42 3RH. Tel/Fax: (01344) 886832. Website: www.uscs.co.uk. (FOPDAC) **USA**.

Heading Away Ltd, 151 Lower Church Road, Burgess Hill, West Sussex. Tel: (01444) 250264. Fax: (01444) 246244. Website: www.headingaway.com. **Malta**.

Hellas Helvetia, 80 Queensway, London W2 3RL. Tel: (020) 7221 5036. Fax: (020) 7229 6339. Website: www.hellas-helvetia.com. (NAEA) **Greece**.

Hodders Sales & Lettings, 186 High Street, Harlesden, London NW10 4ST. Tel: (020) 8965 9878. Fax: (020) 8961 5164. Website: www.hodders.co.uk. (NAEA) **Cyprus**.

Holloway, 35 South Street, Bridport, Dorset DT6 3NY. Tel/

Fax: (01308) 422121. (NAEA) **France**.

Holmes, 195 Reepham Road, Helledon, Norwich NR6 5NZ. Tel: (01603) 484661. Fax: (01603) 482429. (NAEA) **Spain**.

Homes in Spain, 52–54 Pembroke Road, Clifton, Bristol BS8 2DT. Tel: (01452) 312264. Fax: (01454) 315080. E-mail: homesinspain@btinternet.com. **Spain (including Balearics)**.

Ian Tonge Property Services, 152 Buxton Road, High Lane, Stockport, Cheshire SK6 8EA. Tel: (01663) 762677. Fax: (01663) 76253. Website: www.iantongue.co.uk. (NAEA) **Italy, Portugal, Spain (including Balearics and Canary Islands), USA: Florida**.

International Homes, 3 King Street, Mirfield, West Yorks WF14 8AW. Tel/Fax: (01924) 489818. Website: www.international-homes-yorks.co.uk. (NAEA) **Spain**.

IPC Property Consultants Ltd, 38 Church Street, Seaford, East Sussex BN25 1LD. Tel: (01323) 899204. Fax: (01323) 899210. Website: www.ipc-homes.com. (FOPDAC) **Spain (Costa Blanca, Costa del Sol), Canary Islands, Portugal, Bahamas, Barbados**.

J J Properties Abroad, 57 Chapel Street, Petersfield, Hants GU32 3EA. Tel: (01730) 301989. Fax: (01730) 301985. Website: www.jjproperties.co.uk. (FOPDAC) **Spain: Costa Blanca**.

John Fisk & Co, 146 London Road, Benfleet, Essex SS7 5SQ. Tel: (01268) 565555. Fax: (01268) 566291. Website: www.fisks.co.uk. **South Africa**.

Joshua Jacob & Partners, 6 Oxford Street, Nottingham NG1 5BH. Tel: (0115) 910 1387. Fax: (0115) 910 1151. Website: www.jjpi.co.uk. (NAEA) **Spain**.

KBM Consultancy, Unit C, The Mallards, Broadway Lane, South Cerney, Glos GL7 5TQ. Tel: (08700) 113141. Fax: (08700) 113242. Website: www.kbmconsultancy.com. **France**.

Kent Estate Agencies, 99 Mortimer Street, Herne Bay, Kent CT6 5ER. Tel/Fax: (01227) 367441. Website: kent-estate-agencies.co.uk. (NAEA) **Spain**.

Lacey & Co, PO Box 1915, Leigh on Sea, Essex SS9 5NA. Tel: (01702) 603210. Fax: (01702) 603211. Website: www.laceypropertybrokers.com. (FOPDAC) **Spain**

(including Balearics), Portugal, Malta, Greece (including Greek islands).

Latitudes, Grosvenor House, 1 High Street, Edgware, Middlesex HA8 7TA. Tel: (020) 8951 5155. Fax: (020) 8951 5156. Website: www.latitudes.co.uk. (FOPDAC) **France**.

Links French Property Services, Cinnabar, 53 Mowbray Drive, Leighton Buzzard LU7 7PH. Tel: (01525) 372519. Website: www.links-property.co.uk. **France**.

Living-Cyprus.Com, The Leas, 35 Oaklea Mews, Aycliffe, Co Durham DL5 6JP. Tel: (07050) 262576. Fax: (08701) 392693. Website: www.living-cyprus.com. **Cyprus**.

Maison Individuelle, Contract House, 27 Hyde Way, Welwyn Garden City, Herts AL7 3UQ. Tel: (01707) 376255. Fax: (01707) 376250. Website: www.maison-individuelle.co.uk. **France**.

Marjon International, 38 Church Street, Seaford, East Sussex BN25 1LD. Tel: (01323) 892337. Fax: (01323) 899210. Mobile: 07939 543181. E-mail: john.creamer@talk21.com. (FOPDAC) **Portugal (Lisbon and Algarve), Spain, Canary Islands, France (Paris and South)**.

Martins Property Services Ltd, 29 Billet Lane, Hornchurch, Essex RM11 1XP. Tel: (01708) 456126. Fax: (01708) 446238. (NAEA) **Spain**.

Masa International UK Ltd, Airport House, Purley Way, Croydon, Surrey CR0 0XZ. Tel: (020) 8781 1995. Fax: (020) 8781 1920. Website: www.masainter.com. (FOPDAC). **Spain: Costa Blanca**.

MGB Homes International, 8 Exchange Quay, Salford, Manchester M5 3ES. Tel: (0161) 932 1012. Fax: (0161) 932 1210. Website: www.mgbhomes.com. **Spain**.

Morris & Co, Principals House, 21 Stonnall Road, Aldridge, West Midlands WS9 8JX. Tel/Fax: (01922) 744459. Website: www.morris-enterprises.co.uk. (FOPDAC) **Spain: Costa Blanca, Cyprus**.

North & West France Properties, Park Lodge, Park Road, East Twickenham TW1 2PT. Tel: (020) 8891 1750. Fax: (020) 8891 1760. Website: www.all-france-properties.com. **France**.

Overseas-Properties.com, Brunel House, 44 Newton Road,

Torquay TQ2 6AA. Tel: (01803) 290004. Fax: (01803) 290084. Website: www.overseas-properties.com.

Overseas Property Centres, 43 Old Street, Clevedon, Bristol BS21 6DA. Tel: (08712) 221078. Fax: (08712) 221079. **France: Paris and South**.

Papillon Properties, Woodside Cootage, Catmere End, Saffron Walden, Essex CB11 4XG. Tel/Fax: (01799) 527809. **France: Poitou-Charentes region**.

Paul Wright, 121 Ipswich Street, Stowmarket, Suffolk IP14 1BB. Tel: (01449) 613678. Fax: (01449) 774188. Website: www.paulwright.co.uk. (NFEA). **Portugal, Spain**.

Philip Lockwood UK & Overseas, 71 Coventry Street, Kidderminster, Worcs DY10 2BS. Tel/Fax: (01562) 745082. E-mail: phillock@aol.com. (FOPDAC and NAEA) **Spain (including Balearics), Canary Islands, Portugal, France, Malta, Cyprus**.

Pilgrim UK Ltd, 9 High Street, Oakham, Rutland LE15 6AH. Tel: (01572) 756577. Fax: (01572) 722977. Website: wwwpilgrimhomes.com. (FOPDAC) **USA: Florida, Spain: Costa Blanca, Costa del Sol**.

Portico Properties S L, The Springboard Centre, Mantle Lane, Coalville, Leicestershire LE67 3DW. Tel: (01530) 839531. Fax: 01530 810231. Website: www.porticoproperties.com. (NAEA) **Canary Islands: Tenerife**.

Powell & Partners, 39 Station Road East, Oxted, Surrey. Tel: (01883) 712315. Fax: (01883) 730159. E-mail: powelland@aol.com. (NAEA) **Northern France, USA**.

Premier Property Services, 216 Moss Lane, Bramhall, Cheshire SK7 2PB. Tel/Fax: (0161) 439 1626. (FOPDAC) **Spain**.

Prestige Properties and Travel, Prestige House, Radford Business Centre, Radford Crescent, Billericay, Essex CM12 0BZ. Tel: (01277) 652628. Fax: (01277) 632499. Website: www.prestige-group.co.uk. (FOPDAC) **USA: Florida**.

Prime Property International, Moyle House, Fleet Hill, Finchampstead, Berks RG40 4LJ. Tel: (0118) 973 7093. Fax: (0118) 973 6944. (FOPDAC) **Spain: Costa Blanca and Costa del Sol, Portugal**.

Propertunities, 13–17 Newbury Street, Wantage OX12 8BU.
Tel: (01235) 772345. Website: www.propertunities.co.uk.
Spain.

Property Link, 448–450 Bordesley Green, Birmingham B9
5NS. Tel: (0121) 772 8200. Fax: (0121) 766 6474. (NAEA)
USA: Florida.

Property Matters, 16 Market Street, Dartford, Kent DA1
1ET. Tel: (01322) 280100. Fax: (01322) 284664. (NAEA)
Spain.

Quadrant Property Services, 6 Woodlands Road, Camberley,
Surrey GU15 3LZ. Tel: (01276) 507513. Fax: (01276)
507514. (FOPDAC) **Portugal: Algarve, Madeira**.

Rainbow Estates, 45 Gower Street, London WC1E 6NA. Tel:
(020) 7637 4805. Fax: (020) 7580 2067. **Portugal (including
Madeira)**.

Real Crete Properties, Mallories, Stanton St John, Oxon
OX33 1HF. Tel/Fax: (01865) 351056. **Greece: Crete**.

Roger McGhee, 74 St Thomas Street, Weymouth DT4 8EL.
Tel: (01305) 779655. Fax: (01305) 778730. Website:
www.rogermcghee.co.uk. (NAEA) **Spain: Costa Blanca**.

Salter Rex, Crown House, 265–267 Kentish Town Road,
London NW5 2TP. Tel: (020) 7482 4488. Fax: (020) 7485
8488. E-mail: residential@salter-rex.co.uk. (NAEA)
Portugal, West Indies.

Simon Andrew, 621 Washwood Heath Road, Ward End,
Birmingham B8 2HB. Tel: (0121) 328 9999. Fax: (0121) 328
9191. Website: www.propertylive.co.uk. (NAEA) **USA**.

Simmonds en France, PO Box 1737, Fordingbridge, Hants
SP6 3QN. Tel: (01425) 653355. Fax: (0870) 705 8458.
Website: www.enfrance.co.uk. (NAEA) **France (W)**.

Sinclair Overseas Property Network, The Business Centre, PO
Box 492, Leighton Buzzard LU7 7WG. Tel and Fax:
(01525) 375319. Fax: (01525) 851418. **France**.

Small & Partners, 10 Southgate Street, Winchester SO23 9EF.
Tel: (01962) 865250. Fax: (01962) 865757. E-mail:
enquiries@smallandpartners.co.uk. (NAEA) **Spain: Costa
Blanca**.

Sunshine Villas, 9 Weech Road, West Hampstead, London
NW6 1DL. Tel: (020) 7794 9013. Fax: (020) 7794 0256. E-

mail: sunvillas@aol.com. (FOPDAC) **Spain: Costa Blanca**.

The Property Shop, 2 The Square, Thorpe Marriott, Norfolk NR8 6UT. Tel: (01603) 260700. Fax: (01603) 280606. Website: www.property-shop.co.uk. (NAEA) **France**.

Thetford Property, Pal House, Market Place, Thetford, Norfolk IP24 2AL. Tel: (01842) 753388. Fax: (01842) 762093. Website: www.thetfordproperty.co.uk (NAEA) **Spain: Costa Blanca**.

Trevor Kent, Kent House, Oxford Road, Gerrards Cross, Bucks SL9 7DP. Tel: (01753) 885522. Fax: (01753) 887777. Website: www.trevorkent.com. (NAEA) **USA**.

Ultra Villas, 1 Crescent Terrace, Cheltenham GL50 3PE. Tel: (01242) 221500. (FOPDAC) **Spain: Costa Blanca, Portugal**.

Villas Abroad, 100a High Street, Hampton, Middlesex TW12 2ST. Tel: (020) 8941 4499. Fax: (020) 8941 0202. Website: www.fopdac.com. (FOPDAC) **Andorra, France: Riviera, Switzerland**.

Villas Abroad, 53 North Walsham Road, Norwich. Tel: (01603) 412200. Fax: (01603) 412111. Website: www.villas-abroad-online.com. (NAEA) **Bahamas, Cyprus, France, Gibraltar, Italy, Portugal, Spain**.

Wessex Homes, 57 Susans Road, Eastbourne, East Sussex BN21 3TG. Tel: (01323) 749007. Fax: (01323) 749009. Website: www.search1.co.uk/wessex homes. (NAEA) **Gibraltar, Spain**.

Woodvale, Little Venice Parade, 227 Edgware Road, London W2 1TH. Tel: (020) 7224 9900. Fax: (020) 7224 9911. Website: www.woodvale-estates.com. **Cyprus**.

Worldwide Investments, Inc, 26 Chapel Lane, Barwick-in-Elmet, Leeds LS15 4EJ. Tel: (0113) 393 5251. Website: www.wwinvestments.com. **USA**.

Worldwide Property Consultants, PO Box 146, Letchworth, Herts SG6 4PS. Tel: (01526) 830721 (UK), 00 34 950 132880 (Spain). Fax: (01462) 636769. Mobile: 00 34 676 773303. (FOPDAC) **Spain (including Balearics, Canary Islands), Italy (including Sardinia), Greece (including Crete), Cyprus, Portugal**.

Your Place in the Sun, Idvies House, Idvies by Forfar, Angus DD8 2QJ. Tel: (01307) 818787. Fax: (01307) 818933.

Website: www.yourplaceinthesun.org.uk. (FOPDAC) **Spain**.

ESTATE AGENTS (ABROAD)

Angela Pick, 29 rue Sigalon, BP 28, 30700 Uzes, France. Tel:
00 33 4 6622 6320. Fax: 00 33 4 6603 0669. E-mail:
pickprop@club-internet.fr. **France: Gard region**.

Bougainvillea Properties, Barreiras Brancas, 8100-227 Loule,
Portugal. Tel: 00 351 289 413199. Fax: 00 351 289 462666.
E-mail: bougainvillea@mail.telepac.pt. **Portugal**.

Cassar & Cooper, St Anne Court, Tigne Seafront, PO Box 36,
Sliema, Malta. Tel: 00 356 343730. Fax: 00 356 334374.
Website: www.cassar-cooper.com. **Malta**.

Concay Inmobiliarias, Edificio Ignazu, Calle Enrique Talg,
38400 Puerta de la Cruz, Tenerife. Tel: 00 34 922 371452.
Fax: 00 34 922 372106. Website: www.immobilienteneriffa.
com. (FOPDAC) **Spain: Tenerife**.

Conseil Patromoine, 52 Boulevard Victor Hugo, 06000 Nice,
France. Tel: 00 33 4 9703 0333. Mobile: 00 33 6 1542 6721.
France: Paris, Alps, Côte d'Azur.

Contempo, Contempo Plaza, 4713 US Highway 27N,
Davenport, Florida, USA. Tel: 00 1 863 424 0219. Fax: 00
1 863 424 0219 and 00 1 863 424 8965. Website:
www.contempogroup.com. **USA: Florida**.

Country Casas International SL, Avenida Oeste 8, La Jara,
03700 Denia (Alicante), Spain. Tel/Fax: 00 34 96 642 5101.
E-mail: countrycasas@wanadoo.es. (FOPDAC and NAEA)
Spain: Costa Blanca.

David Russell, Pedro Mesquida, Padeo Maritimo 12, Palma
de Mallorca, Spain. Tel: 00 34 971 734073. Fax: 00 34 971
451565. (FOPDAC) **Spain: Majorca**.

Fincas Andalucia, Calle La Nora 21, 29170 Colmenar
(Malaga), Spain. Tel/Fax: 00 34 952 730570. Mobile: 00 34
670 338582. (FOPDAC) **Spain: Andalucia**.

Guinnard Immobilier et Tourisme SA, Rue du Centre Sportif,
PO Box 214, CH 1936 Verbier, Switzerland. Tel: 00 41 27
771 7107. Fax: 00 41 27 771 7102. Website:
www.guinnard.com. (FOPDAC) **Switzerland**.

Hampton-Fieldings International, Urb La Carolina, Edif Commerical, Ctra Cadiz Km 178 5, Marbella 29600. Tel: 00 34 95 282 7754. Fax: 00 34 95 282 9754. Website: www.fielding-esp.com. (NAEA) **Spain**.

Homefinders & Properties Direct, Cantheil, 14770 St Vigor des Mezerets, France. Tel: 00 33 2 3169 0902. Website: www.homefinderseurope.com. (FOPDAC) **France**.

Homenet Property Group, PO Box 317, Pavilion 3611, Kwa Zulu Natal. Tel: 00 27 31 266 9850. Fax: 00 27 31 266 8494. Website: www.homenet.co.za. (NAEA) **South Africa**.

Horizon Property Group, Local No 25, Edificio Don Antonia, No19 Calle Juan XXIII, Los Cristianos, Arona, Tenerife. Tel/Fax: 00 34 922 792651. Website: www.tenerife-estateagents.com. (FOPDAC) **Spain: Tenerife**.

Images of Andalucia, Tara, Cortijo del Roble, Carboneras, Villaneuva del Rosario, 29312 Malaga, Spain. Tel/Fax: 00 34 211 1178. Website: www.imagesofandalucia.com. **Spain: south**.

International Property Assistance, Cami de la Mar 30-8, 3580 Alfaz del Pi, Alicante, Spain. Tel: 00 34 965 887696. Fax: 00 34 966 860136. Website: www.ipa.nl. **Spain: Costa Blanca**.

Leana Nel Homes, PO Box 78201, Sandton 2146, South Africa. Tel: 00 27 11 706 4222. Fax: 00 27 11 706 4401. Website: www.propertiessouthafrica.com. **South Africa**.

Leggett Immobilier, 224340 La Rochebeaucourt, France. Tel: 00 33 5 5356 6254. Fax: 00 33 5 5356 6257. Website: frenchestateagents.com. **France: SW**.

Martin Mundy Property Sales & Management, Calle Saint Pere Baix 5, 17480 Roses, Girona, Spain. Tel: 00 34 972 257970. Fax: 00 34 972 254499. (FOPDAC) **Spain: Costa Brava**.

Molino Villas Servicios Inmobilarios SL, Centro Commercial Kristal Mar No 18c, 03724 Moraira-Teulada (Alicante), Spain. Tel: 00 34 966 492335. Fax: 00 34 966 492012. Website: www.molinovillas.com. (FOPDAC) **Spain: Costa Blanca**.

Ocean Estates, Avenida de Rivera, 3 Puerto Banus, Marbella, 29880 Malaga, Spain. Tel: 00 34 952 811750. Fax: 00 34

952 906446. **Spain: Costa del Sol**.

Pam Golding Properties, 50 Long Street, Cnr Long and Hout Streets, Cape Town, South Africa. Tel: 00 27 21 419 4999. (UK representative: FPD Savills) **South Africa**.

Real Estate Connection Inc, 1959 Lee Road, Suite 125, Winter Park, FL 32789, USA. Tel: 00 1 407 740 7855. Fax: 00 1 407 740 7920. Website: www.cflvachomes.com. **USA: Florida**.

Tenerife Property Shop, Local 117, Puerto Colon, Playa de las Americas, Tenerife, Canary Islands. Tel: 00 34 922 714700. Fax: 00 34 922 715720. Website: www.tenerifepropertyshop.com. **Canary Islands: Tenerife**.

Tuscan Homes, Via Pontevecchio 10, Barga (LU), Italy. Tel: 00 39 583 711225. Fax: 00 39 583 724042. Website: www.tuscanhomes.com. **Italy**.

Unwin Estates, PO Box 768, Girne, North Cyprus via Mersin 10, Turkey. Tel: 00 90 392 822 3508. Website: www.unwinestates.com. **Northern Cyprus**.

Villaman, Via di Tuglio 433, 55100 Lucca, Italy. Tel/Fax: 00 39 0583 464591. Mobile: 00 39 3485 110416. Website: www.villaman.com. (FOPDAC). **Italy: Tuscany**.

Whistler Real Estate Co, 137-4379 Lorimer Road, Whistler, British Columbia, Canada V0N 1B4. Tel: 00 1 604 932 5538. Website: www.wrec.com. (NAEA). **Canada**.

FINANCE

The firms below specialise in various aspects of finance, such as investment, mortgages, currency transfer, pensions or tax planning.

Blevins Franks Financial Management, Barbican House, 26–34 Old Street, London EC1V 9QQ. Tel: (020) 7336 1111. Fax: (020) 7336 1100. Website: www.blevinsfranks.com.

Conti Financial Services, 204 Church Road, Hove, East Sussex BN3 2DJ. Tel: (01273) 772811. Fax: (01273) 321269. Website: www.overseasandukfinance.com. (FOPDAC) Mortgages.

Continental Financial Practice Ltd, 204 Church Road, Hove, East Sussex BN3 2DJ. Tel: (01273) 820458. Fax: (01273) 820478.

Currencies Direct, Hanover House, 73–74 High Holborn, London WC1V 6LR. Tel: (020) 7813 0332. Fax: (020) 7419 7753.

Expatriate Advisory Services PLC, 14 Gordon Road, West Bridgeford, Nottingham NG2 5LN. Tel: (0115) 981 6572.

Wilfred T Fry Ltd, Crescent House, Crescent Road, Worthing, Sussex BN11 1RN. Tel: (01903) 231545. Fax: (01903) 200868.

Moneycorp Commercial Foreign Exchange, 2 Sloane Street, Knightsbridge, London SW1A 9LA. Tel: (020) 7235 4200. Fax: (020) 7235 4250. Website: www.moneycorp.co.uk.

PKF (Guernsey) Ltd, PO Box 296, St Peter Port, Guernsey GY1 1DZ. Tel: 01481 727927. Fax: (01481) 710511. Website: www.pkfguernsey.com. Financial planning for expatriates in France and Spain.

Society of Pensions Consultants, St Bartholomew House, 92 Fleet Street, London EC4. Tel: (020) 7353 1688. Fax: (020) 7353 9296.

TSW International, 1st Floor, Jupiter House, Station Road, Cambridge CB1 2JZ. Tel: (01223) 363650. Tax and financial planning consultants.

UK Expatriates Professional Advisory Services Ltd, 84 Grange Road, Middlesborough TS1 2LS. Tel: (01642) 221211.

Www.mortgages-in-spain.com, PO Box 146, Ilkley, W Yorks LS29 8UL. Tel: (0800) 027 7057. Fax: (0845) 345 6586.

GOVERNMENT DEPARTMENTS

Benefits Agency, Overseas Branch, Benton Park Road, Newcastle upon Tyne NE98 1YX. Tel: (0191) 213 5000.

Department of the Environment, Food and Rural Affairs: Export of Cats and Dogs Section, 1A Page Street, London SW1P 4PQ. Tel: (020) 7904 6347. PETS helpline: (0870) 241 1710.

Website: www.defra.gov.uk/animalh/quarantine.

Email: pets.helpline@defra.gsi.gov.uk

Department of Health International Branch, Room 512, Richmond House, 79 Whitehall, London SW1A 2NS. Website: www.doh.gov.uk/traveladvice. Information on eligibility to state health facilities abroad.

Department of Health Leaflets Unit, PO Box 21, Honeypot Lane, Stanmore, Middx HA7 1AY. Tel: (0800) 555777.

Inland Revenue Claims Branch (Foreign Division), Merton Road, Bootle L69 9BL. Website: www.inlandrevenue.gov.uk.

Inland Revenue FICO (Non-residents), St John's House, Merton Road, Bootle, Merseyside L69 9BB. Tel: (0151) 472 6208.

Inland Revenue (Inspector of Foreign Dividends), 72 Maid Marian Way, Nottingham NG1 6AS. Tel: (01602) 242299.

Inland Revenue Public Departments (Foreign Section), Ty-Glas, Llanishen, Cardiff CF4 5WN. Tel: (0222) 753271.

National Insurance Contributions Office, International Services, Benton Park Road, Newcastle upon Tyne. Tel: (0191) 225 4811. Website: www.inlandrevenue.gov.uk/nic/index.htm

Passport Agency (UK). Tel: (0870) 521 0410.

Clive House, 70 Petty France, SW1H 9HD. Personal callers only.

5th Floor, India Buildings, Water St, Liverpool L2 0QZ. Serves North of England and North Wales.

Olympia House, Upper Dock St, Newport NP1 1XA. Serves South Wales, South and West of England.

Aragon Court, Northminster Road, Peterborough PE1 1QG. Serves Midlands, East Anglia, Kent.

3 Northgate, 96 Milton Street, Cowcaddens, Glasgow G4 0BT. Serves Scotland, London, Middlesex.

Hampton House, 47–53 High Street, Belfast BT1 2QS. Serves Northern Ireland.

Pensions Info-line: (08457) 731 3233.

The Pension Service, Overseas Pensions Department, Newcastle upon Tyne, NE98 1BA. Tel: (0191) 228 7777. Website: www.dss.gov.uk.

Social Security Agency, Overseas Branch, Lindsay House, 8–14 Callender Street, Belfast BT1 5DP (Northern Ireland only).

HOLIDAYS

Cosmos Golden Times, Tourama House, 17 Homesdale Road, Bromley, Kent BR2 9LX. Tel: (0870) 901 0790. Website: www.cosmos-holidays.co.uk.

Crystal Holidays, Kings Place, 12–42 Wood Street, Kingston on Thames KT1 1JY. Tel: (020) 8939 5126. Website: www.crystal.com.

Cunard Line Ltd, South Western House, Canute Road, Southampton S09 1ZA. Tel: (023) 802 9933. Website: www.cunard.com.

Fred Olsen Cruises Ltd, Fred Olsen House, White House Road, Ipswich IP1 5LL. Tel: (01473) 292200. Website: www.fredolsen.co.uk.

Home Base Holidays, 7 Park Avenue, London N13 5PG. Tel: (020) 8886 8752. Website: www.homebase-hols.com.

Homelink International, Linfield House, Gorse Hill Road, Virginia Water, Surrey GU25 4AS. Tel: (01344) 842642. Website: www.homelink.org.uk.

Intervac Home Exchange, Coxes Hill Barn, North Wroxall, Chippenham, Wilts SN14 7AD. Tel: (01225) 892208. Website: www.intervac.co.uk.

Organisation for Timeshare in Europe (OTE), 15–19 Great Titchfield Street, London W1P 7FB. Tel: (020) 7291 0901.

Saga Holidays, The Saga Building, Middleburg Square, Folkestone CT20 1AZ. Tel: (0800) 300456. Website: www.sagaholidays.com.

Thomson Young at Heart, Greater London House, Hampstead Road, London NW1 7SD. Tel: (020) 7387 9321. Website: www.thomson-holidays.co.uk.

Timeshare Consumers' Association, Hodsock, Worksop, Notts S81 0TF. Tel: (01909) 591100. Website: www.timeshare.org.uk.

Villa Owners Club (Holiday Property Bond), HPB House,

Newmarket, Suffolk CB8 8EH. Tel: (01638) 660066.

INSURANCE

BUPA International, Russell Mews, Brighton BN7 2NE. Tel: (01273) 208181. Website: www.bupa-intl.com.

Dave Tester Expatriate Insurance Services, 18a Hove Park Villas, Hove BN3 6HG. Tel: (01273) 703469. Fax: (01273) 777723. E-mail: info@expatriate-insurance.com.

Exeter Friendly Society, Beech Hill House, Walnut Gardens, Exeter EX4 4DG. Tel: (01392) 498063. Health insurance.

Goodhealth International Healthcare, 5 Lloyds Avenue, London EC3N 3AE. Tel: (0870) 442 7376. Website: www.goodhealth.co.uk. Medical insurance.

Healthsearch Ltd, 9 Newland Street, Rugby CV22 7BJ. Tel: (01788) 541855. Impartial advice on healthcare plans.

International Private Healthcare Ltd, PO Box 488, IPH House, Borehamwood, Herts WD6 4AN. Tel: (020) 8905 2888.

London and European Title Insurance Services Ltd, Blagrave House, 17 Blagrave Street, Reading RG1 1PW. Tel: (0118) 957 5000.

Private Patients Plan, Philips House, Crescent Road, Tunbridge Wells TN1 2PL. Tel: (01892) 772002.

Woodham Group, 17 Fircroft Close, Woking, Surrey GU22 7LZ. Tel: (01483) 770787. Fax: (01483) 750302.

LANGUAGE LEARNING

Association for Language Learning, 150 Railway Terrace, Rugby CV21 2PN. Tel: (01788) 546443.
Website: www.all-languages.org.uk

Audio Forum, Microworld House, 2–6 Foscote Mews. London W6 2HH. Tel: (020) 7262 2178. Website: www.microworld@ndirect.co.uk. Self-instruction language courses.

Berlitz Language Centres, 296–302 High Holborn, London WC1 7JH. Tel: (020) 7611 9640. Website: www.berlitz.com

Cambridge Advisory Service, Rectory Lane, Kinston, Cambridge CB3 7NL. Tel: (01223) 264089. Language courses abroad.

CESA, Western House, Malpas, Truro, Cornwall TR1 1SQ. Tel: (01872) 225300. Website: www.cesalanguages.com. Language courses abroad.

French Institute, 14 Cromwell Place, London SW7 2JR. Tel: (020) 7581 2701. (Also in Edinburgh.) French courses.

Grant & Cutler, 55–57 Great Marlborough Street, London W1V 2AY. Tel: (020) 7734 2012. Language bookshop.

Hispanic & Luzo Brazilian Council, Canning House, 2 Belgrave Square, London SW1X 8PJ. Tel: (020) 7235 2303. Portuguese courses.

Institute of Linguists, 48 Southwark Street, London SE1 1UN. Tel: (020) 7940 3100. Website: www.iol.org.uk.

Italian Institute, 39 Belgrave Square, London SW1X 8NX. Tel: (020) 7823 1887. Italian courses.

LCL, 104 Judd Street, London WC1H 9NF. Tel: (071) 837 0487. Language bookshop.

Linguaphone Institute, 124 Brompton Road, London SW3. Tel: (020) 7589 2422.

Linguarama, 7th Floor, BPP House, 70 Red Lion Street, London WC1R 4NG. Tel: (020) 7405 7557. Website: linguarama.com. Language tuition.

SIBS, West Wing, Fen Drayton House, 5 Park Lane, Fen Drayton, Cambridgeshire CB4 5SW. Tel: (01954) 231956. Language courses abroad.

Spanish (Cervantes) Institute, 102 Eaton Square, London SW1. Tel: (020) 7245 0621. Spanish courses.

For a more extensive list of language training providers please consult *How to Master Languages* (How To Books).

LEGAL SERVICES

The following UK-based practices are able to undertake conveyancing and other legal services (including wills) in the countries designated.

Baily Gibson, 5 Station Parade, Beaconsfield, Bucks HP9
2PG. Tel: (01494) 672661. Fax: (01494) 678493. Website:
www.bailygibson.co.uk. (FOPDAC) **Spain**.

Bennett & Co, 144 Knutsford Road, Wilmslow, Cheshire SK9
6JP. Tel: (01625) 586937. Fax: (01625) 585362. **Caribbean,
Cyprus, France, Greece, Portugal, Spain, Turkey**.

Castaldi Mourre Sprague, Royalty House, 32 Sackville Street,
London W1X 3EA. Tel: (020) 7432 6160. Fax: (020) 7432
6190. E-mail: cmsuk@castaldimourre.com. (FOPDAC)
France, Italy.

Cornish & Co, Lex House, 1/7 Hainault Street, Ilford IG1
4EL. Tel: (020) 8478 3300. Fax: (020) 8553 3418.
(FOPDAC) **Gibraltar, Spain, Portugal**.

Croft Baker & Co, 95 Aldwych, London WC2B 4JF. Tel:
(020) 7395 4303. Fax: (020) 7395 4304. E-mail:
baker@johnvenn.co.uk. (FOPDAC) **France, Switzerland**.

De Pinna, 35 Piccadilly, London W1V 0PJ. Tel: (020) 7208
2900. Fax: (020) 7208 0066. Website: www.depinna.co.uk.
Spain.

Fernando Scornik Gerstein, 32 St James' Street, London
SW1A 1HD. Tel: (020) 7839 1581. **Spain**.

Florez-Valcarcel, 130 King Street, London W6 0QU. Tel/Fax:
(020) 8741 4867. **Spain**.

Henry C F Fowkes, Fowkes & Son, 12 Western Road,
Romford, Essex RM1 3QA. Tel: (01708) 721611. **France**.

Dr Giovanni Lombardo, Warford Court, 29 Throgmorton
Street, London EC2N 2AT. Tel: (020) 7256 7467. Fax:
(020) 7256 7466. **Italy**.

Graham Platt, Bank House, 150 Roundhay Road, Leeds L58
5LD. Tel: (0113) 209 8922. **France**.

Hugh James Jones & Jenkins (D C W Preece), Arlbee House,
Greyfriars Road, Cardiff CF1 4BQ. Tel: (02920) 224871.
France, Germany, Italy, Spain.

Javier de Juan, 28b Greyhound Road, London W6 8NX. Tel:
(020) 7381 0470. Fax: (020) 7381 4155. Website:
www.spanishlaw.org.uk. **Spain**.

John Howell & Co, 17 Maiden Lane, Covent Garden, London
WC2E 7NA. Tel: (020) 7420 0400. Fax: (020) 7836 3626.
Website: www.legal21.org. (FOPDAC) **Spain, Portugal,**

Norway, Malta, France, Ireland, Italy, Greece, Germany, Cyprus, Austria.
Lita Gale, 43–45 Gower Street, London WC1E 6HH. Tel: (020) 7580 2066. Fax: (020) 7580 2067. **Portugal**.
Neville de Rougemont & Associates, City Cloisters, Suite C4, 188–196 Old Street, London EC1V 8BP. Tel: (020) 7490 4656. Fax: (020) 7490 4417. **Portugal**.
Pannone & Partners, 123 Deansgate, Manchester M2 2BU. Tel: (0161) 909 3000. Fax: (0161) 909 4444. **Andorra, France, Italy, Spain, Portugal, Switzerland**.
Sean O'Connor & Co, 2 River Walk, Tonbridge, Kent TN9 1DT. Tel: (01732) 365378. Fax: (01732) 360144. **France**.
Turner & Co, 6th Floor, Beaufort House, Birmingham B3 1PB. Tel: (0121) 200 1612. Fax: (0121) 200 1613. **France**.

REMOVALS

Below is a select list of firms which specialise in international removals, some of which have branches or agents across the UK. The British Association of Removers (3 Churchill Court, 58 Station Road, North Harrow HA2 7SA. Tel: (020) 8861 3331), which operates a bonding scheme, can suggest firms in your particular area.

Amertrans, Bushey Mill Lane, Watford WD2 4JG. Tel: (01923) 54444.
Armishaws International Removals, Wincanton Business Park, Wincanton, Somerset BA9 9RT. Tel: (01963) 34065. Fax: (01963) 34075.
ARTS International, Ditchling Common Industrial Estate, Hassocks, Sussex BN6 8SL. Tel: (01444) 247551. Fax: (01444) 870072.
Avalon Overseas, Drury Way, Brent Park, London NW10 0JN. Tel: (020) 8451 6336. Fax: (020) 8451 6419. Website: www.avalon-overseas.com.
Bishops Move, Overseas House, Stewarts Road, London SW8 4UG. Tel: (020) 7501 4954. Fax: (020) 7498 0749. Website: www.bishops-move.co.uk.

Britannia International Removals, Unit 3, Wyvern Estate, New Malden, Surrey KT3 4PH. Tel: (0845) 600 6661. Fax: (020) 8336 0961. Website: www.britannia-movers.co.uk.

Callington Carriers, Valentine Road, Callington, Cornwall PL17 7DF. Tel: (01579) 383210. Fax: (01579) 384290.

Copsey Removals, 178 Crow Lane, Romford, Essex RM7 0ES. Tel: (020) 8592 1003. Fax: 01708 727305.

Cotswold Carriers, Warehouse 2, The Walk, Hook, Hook Norton Road, Chipping Norton, Oxon OX7 5TG. Tel: (01608) 730500. Website: www.cotswoldcarriers.co.uk.

Davies Turner, 334 Queenstown Road, London SW8 4HG. Tel: (020) 7622 9361.

Doree Bonner International, International House, Rochester Way, Dartford, Kent DA1 3QY. Tel: (020) 8690 2185. Website: www.doreebonner.co.uk.

Galleon International Shipping Co Ltd, Galleon House, Kerry Avenue, Purfleet Industrial Park, Aveley, Essex RM15 4YA. Tel: (01708) 868068.

H Appleyard & Sons, Denby Way, Hellaby Industrial Estate, Rotherham, S Yorks. Tel: (01709) 549718.

Metro Removals, Orion Way, Kettering, Northants NN15 6NL. Tel: (01536) 519450.

Overs International, Unit 8, Government Road Retail Park, Aldershot GU11 2DA. Tel: (01252) 343646. Fax: (01252) 345861.

PSS International Removals, 8 Redcross Way, London SE1 9HR. Tel: (020) 7407 6606. Website: www.p-s-s.co.uk.

Simpson's of Sussex, Units 1,2,3, Tidy Industrial Estate, Ditchling Common, Hassocks, East Sussex TN6 1JU. Tel: (08000) 271958. Fax: (01444) 247400.

Roy Trevor, Knutsford Road, Warrington, Cheshire WA4 1JE. Tel: (01925) 630441. Website: www.roy-trevor.com.

The Old House, 15/17 High Street, Seaford, East Sussex. Tel: (020) 8947 1817. Website: www.amsmoving.co.uk.

Appendix D
Bibliography

BOOKS

Allied Dunbar Retirement Planning Handbook, David Bertram (Financial Times).
Daily Telegraph Guide to Living Abroad, Michael Furnell (Kogan Page).
The Directory (European Council of International Schools).
Good Non-Retirement Guide, Rosemary Brown (Enterprise Dynamics/Kogan Page).
Getting a Job Abroad, Roger Jones (How To Books).
Have a Happy and Healthy Retirement, Michael Apple (Hodder & Stoughton).
Health and Illness in Retirement, Anne Roberts (Ace Books).
How to Master Languages, Roger Jones (How To Books).
Lett's Retirement Guide, Douglas Shields (Isis).
Life in the Sun, Nancy Tuft (Age Concern England).
Money Matters: Retirement and Beyond, Valerie Smart (W Green & Son).
Parents' Guide to Independent Schools (School Fees Insurance Agency).
Pensions Handbook, Sue Ward (Ace Books).
Retirement Abroad, Robert Cooke (Robert Hale).
Successful Retirement, Gill Crawley (Choice Publications).
Sun, Sand & Cement: A Guide to Buying Overseas Property, Cheryl Taylor (Rosters).
The Traveller's Handbook, Carole Brandenburger, ed. (WEXAS, 45 Brompton Road, London SW3 1DE).
Which Guide to an Active Retirement, Jane Vass (Consumers' Association).
Which Guide to Pensions, Jonquil Lowe (Consumers'

Association).
World Directory of Old Age, Centre for Policy on Ageing
(Cartermill).
Your Taxes and Savings, Sally West (Ace Books).

PERIODICALS

Active Life, Lexicon, 1st Floor, 1–5 Clerkenwell Road,
London EC1M 5PA. Tel: (020) 7253 5775.
BBC Worldwide, BBC World Service, PO Box 76, Bush
House, Strand, London WC2B 4PH. Tel: (020) 7240
3456.
Choice, Apex House, Oundle Road, Peterborough PE2 9NP.
Tel: (01733) 555123.
Dalton's Weekly, CI Tower, St George's Square, New
Malden, Surrey KT3 4JA. Tel: (020) 8329 0100. Website:
www.daltons.co.uk.
The Economist, Economist Subscription Fulfilment Service,
PO Box 471, Haywards Heath RG16 3GY. Tel: (01444)
475647. Website:www.economist.com.
Focus on France – see *World of Property* entry.
Good Times, ARP/0050, 4th Floor, Greencoat House,
Francis Street, London SW1P 1DZ. Tel: (020) 7828 0500.
The Guardian Weekly, Guardian Publications Ltd, 164
Deansgate, Manchester M60 2RR. Tel: (0161) 832 7200.
Homes Overseas Magazine, 207 Providence Square, Mill
Street, London SE1 2EW. Tel: (020) 7939 9888. Website:
www.blendoncommunications.co.uk.
International Homes Magazine, 3 St John's Court,
Moulsham Street, Chelmsford CM2 0JD. Tel: (01245)
358877. Website: www.international-homes.com.
Mature Tymes, The Wharf, 121 Schooner Way, Cardiff,
South Glamorgan CF10 4ET.
The Oldie, 45–46 Poland Street, London W1V 4AU. Tel:
(020) 7734 2225.
On Air, BBC World Service, PO Box 76, Bush House,
Strand, London WC2B 4PH. (Monthly overseas radio
and TV programme bulletin.)

Opportunities Abroad, Christians Abroad, Room 233, Bon
   Marche Centre, 241–9 Ferndale Road, London SW9 8BJ.
   Tel: (020) 7346 5950. Monthly bulletin of vacancies in
   voluntary and non-government organisations.
Overseas Jobs Express, Premier House, Shoreham Airport,
   East Sussex, BN43 5FF. Tel: (01273) 440220.
Private Villas, CI Tower, St George's Square, New Malden,
   Surrey KT3 4JA. Tel: (020) 8949 6199. Website:
   www.privatevillas.co.uk.
Resident Abroad, Financial Times Magazines, Maple House,
   Tottenham Court Road, London W1P 9LL. Tel: (020)
   7896 2325.
Saga Magazine, Saga Building, Middleburg Square,
   Folkestone, Kent CT20 1AZ. Tel: (01303) 711526.
The Weekly Telegraph, PO Box 14, Harold Hill, Romford,
   Essex RM3 8EQ. Tel: (01708) 38100.
World of Property Magazine, Outbound Newspapers, 1
   Commercial Road, Eastbourne BN21 3XQ. Tel: (01323)
   726040. Website: www.outboundpublishing.com
Yours, Tower House, Sovereign Park, Market Harborough
   LE16 9EF. Tel: (01733) 555161.

More publications are featured in the individual country
sections.

Index